GRAMMARWORK

4

PAMELA BREYER

ENGLISH EXERCISES IN CONTEXT

PRENTICE HALL REGENTS, Englewood Cliffs, NJ 07632

Book Design: **Suzanne Bennett & Associates**
Project Editor: **Karen Davy**
CREDITS: **Pages 1, 10, 34, 38, 44, 59, 61, 72, 77, 85, 100, illustrations by Erasmo Hernandez. Pages 5, 9, 11, 19, 20, 24, 26, 28, 33, 36, 45, 57, 59, 63, 65, 71, 82, 85, 97, 101, illustrations by Anne Burgess. Pages 6, 12, 21, 32, 46, 54, 62, 76, 78, 83, 87, 90, illustrations by Steven Cavallo. Page 17, photos from New York Convention and Visitors Bureau (top) and New York State Department of Commerce (bottom). Page 47, photo from the collection of Lisa Wolff. Pages 50 and 60, photos © Laimute E. Druskis. Page 67, photo from Hawaii Visitors Bureau. Page 68, photo from United States Department of Housing and Urban Development. Page 75, photo from Phototeque.**

A Division of Simon & Schuster
Englewood Cliffs, NJ 07632

ISBN 0-13-362302-5 01

Printed in the United States of America

10 9 8 7 6 5 4

Prentice-Hall International (UK) Limited, *London*
Prentice-Hall of Australia Pty. Limited, *Sydney*
Prentice-Hall Canada Inc., *Toronto*
Prentice-Hall Hispanoamericana, S.A., *Mexico*
Prentice-Hall of India Private Limited, *New Delhi*
Prentice-Hall of Japan, Inc., *Tokyo*
Simon & Schuster Asia Pte. Ltd., *Singapore*
Editora Prentice-Hall do Brasil, Ltda., *Rio de Janeiro*

To Jennie Speidell
for her ninety-fourth birthday

Contents

Introduction		XI
Nouns		
Regular Noun Plurals: *-s, -es, -ies*	**Irises** and **pansies** are flowers.	1
-S vs. No *-S* with Countable Nouns	It's on a wooded **lot** with **trees** all around it.	2
Possessive of Nouns	Could they be Doris **Gross'** keys?	3
Countable and Uncountable Nouns	**Antiques** and **Architecture**	4
Noun Comparisons with *More, Less,* and *Fewer*	I'd like **more** friends. I'd like **fewer** acquaintances.	5
Noun Comparisons with *Less, The Least, Fewer,* and *The Fewest*	New City has **the fewest** schools of the three.	6, 7
Determiners		
A vs. *An*	**A** university library	8
A and *An* before Adjectives	Are you **a** licensed electrician?	9
No Article vs. *A* and *An*	Snow melts. **An** ice cube melts.	10
A vs. *The*	She walked into **the** bathroom and grabbed **a** toothbrush.	11
No Article vs. *A* or *The*	Shirts were half price. I bought **a** shirt.	12, 13
A vs. *Some*	I'm going to buy **a** broom and **some** kitchen towels.	14
No Article vs. *The* with Expressions of Time and Place	He'll go to school in **the** fall.	15
No Article vs. *The* with Place Names	A trip to **the** Metropolitan Museum and Central Park	16, 17
Pronouns		
Reflexive Pronouns	Madeleine painted the entire kitchen **herself.**	18
Another, The Other, and *The Others*	**The others** are tall.	19
Indefinite Pronouns	**Someone** broke into his apartment.	20
Who's vs. *Whose*	**Whose** jewelry was stolen?	21
They're, There, and the Possessive Adjective *Their*	**There** are no lights on. **They're** not at home.	22

Simple Present Tense		
Subject-Verb Agreement	Heat **costs** $65.70 a month.	23
Subject-Verb Agreement	My husband and I **clean** the house.	24
Make vs. *Do*	I **do** the errands.	25
Simple Form vs. Present Form	She doesn't **make** a lot of money, but she **works** very hard.	26
Subject-Verb Agreement with *There Is* and *There Are*	There **are** excellent cultural events in a big city.	27
Simple Past Tense		
Regular and Irregular Past Tense Verbs	As he **came** in, he **turned** to Mr. Jones and **said,** "Bon appetit."	28, 29
Regular and Irregular Past Tense Verbs	She **wrote** her first book at the age of 24.	30, 31
Simple Form vs. Past Form	She didn't **go** to school.	32
Irregular Past Tense Verbs	I **heard** a funny joke yesterday.	33
Future Time		
Future with *Going To* and *Will*	He**'ll fly** to San Juan, Puerto Rico.	34
Statements with *Before, After, When,* and *As Soon As*	He**'ll do** some shopping when he**'s** in St. Thomas.	35
The Continuous Tenses		
Present Continuous: Subject-Verb Agreement	One of the boys **is sitting** in two seats.	36, 37
Past Continuous: Subject-Verb Agreement	The man behind the two women **was writing** a check.	38
Past Continuous: Statements with *When* and *While*	While she **was watching** television, her two oldest children **came** home from school.	39
Future Continuous: Negative and Affirmative Statements	David **will be bringing** a guest.	40
Present Perfect Continuous	You mean he**'s been raking** the leaves for three hours?	41
The Perfect Tenses		
Present Perfect: Statements with *Already* and *Yet*	No, thanks. I**'ve already had** dinner.	42
Present Perfect: Statements with *Never*	I**'ve never heard** Egyptian music.	43
Present Perfect: Questions with *Ever*	**Have you ever ridden** a camel?	44
Past Perfect: Affirmative Statements	By the time Gary got there, the wedding reception **had started.**	45
Past Perfect: Negative Statements	Until last week, Mario **hadn't seen** snow.	46
Tense Contrast		
Simple Present, Simple Past, and the Future with *Will*	The couple **will reside** in Buckingham.	47

Verb + Infinitive vs. Verb + Gerund	When Kay and Jack were 65 years old, they **decided to retire.**	48
Simple Past vs. Present Perfect	He**'s visited** 143 countries so far. He **visited** 4 countries last summer.	49
Negative and Affirmative Short Answers	Is the stereo absolutely free? **No, it isn't.**	50, 51
Tag Questions	You remember Dee Williams, **don't you?**	52

Conditionals

Future Real Conditional: Affirmative Statements	If you **buy** a new car now, you**'ll get** a rebate.	53
Present Unreal Conditional: Affirmative Statements	If I **were** a bird, I**'d like** to be a swan.	54
Contrast: Present Unreal and Future Real Conditionals	If I **won** a million dollars, I**'d take** a trip around the world.	55
Past Unreal Conditional: Negative and Affirmative Statements	If I **had been** King Edward of England, I **wouldn't have given up** my throne for a woman.	56
Past Unreal Conditional: Negative Statements	If she **hadn't woken up** late, she **wouldn't have been** in a hurry.	57

Modals and Idiomatic Modals

Should vs. *Would Rather*	I **should do** my homework, but I**'d rather read** a book.	58
Have To, Don't Have To, and *Must Not*	You **must not get up** and walk around.	59
Opportunity with *Could*	She **could take** a nap.	60
Possibility with *Could* and *Might*	It **could be** a rainbow. It **might be** a rainbow.	61
Used To	They **used to work** eight hours a day.	62
Be Used To	She **isn't used to living** in the city.	63
Should Have	She **should have taken** her money with her.	64
Past Possibility with *Could Have*	She **could have had** an accident.	65
Contrast: Modal and Verb Form Review	**Could** you **have left** it in your pocket?	66

Passive Voice

Simple Present	This fabulous hotel **is located** right on the beach.	67
Simple Past	The house **was built** in 1841.	68
Active Voice vs. Passive Voice	Her supervisor **was notified** about the accident.	69
Future	Dinner **will be served** at 8:00.	70
Causatives	I **have** my teeth **checked** once a year.	71

Conjunctions

Compound Subjects and Objects	Air pollution comes from automobiles**,** buses**, and** trucks.	72, 73
Compound Sentences with *And, So,* and *But*	He didn't make a good impression in the interview**, so** Mr. Simon isn't going to hire him.	74

Adjectives and Adjectivals

Adjective Comparatives	Variety shows are **more entertaining.**	75
Adjective Superlatives	It has **the most exciting** roller coaster ride in the world.	76, 77
Adjectives Ending in *-ed* and *-ing*	I thought it was **boring.** I was **bored.**	78
Any, *No*, and the Pronoun *None*	There was **no** electricity in Queens.	79
Essential Adjective Clauses with *Who*	I don't like people **who complain all the time.**	80
Verb Agreement in Essential Adjective Clauses with *Which* or *That*	I like houses **which are easy to clean.**	81
Essential Adjective Clauses: *Who* vs. *Which*	I like waiters **who are pleasant.**	82

Adverbs and Adverbials

Adverbs of Manner	I think you work very **hard.**	83
Adjective vs. Adverb	I'm not a very **good** piano player. I can't play the piano very **well.**	84
Adverb Comparatives	He should have practiced **longer.**	85
Adverbial Clauses with *Because* and *Although*	**Because** Ruby works hard**,** she deserves a promotion.	86

Noun Clauses

Clauses with *Hope*	I **hope** she **has** a boy.	87
Clauses with *Wish:* Present Events	I **wish** I **didn't have to** work.	88
Clauses with *Wish:* Past Events	She **wishes** the guests **hadn't arrived** early.	89
Indirect Speech: Noun Clauses from Statements	Her mother said that **she was** too young to get married.	90, 91
Indirect Speech: Infinitive Phrases from Imperatives	His uncle **told him not to get** married now.	92
Indirect Speech: Noun Clauses from Yes-No Questions	The interviewer asked Diane **if she could begin** tomorrow.	93
Indirect Speech: Noun Clauses from Information Questions	The interviewer asked Diane **how fast she could type.**	94
Indirect Speech: Noun Clauses from Yes-No Questions and Information Questions	I can't believe he asked her **if she was** happily **married.**	95

Prepositions

For, Since, and *Ago*	He was sales manager **for** four years.	96
To or *For* vs. No Preposition	She bought gifts **for** her family.	97
Prepositions of Time and Place	He'll stay in Quito **from** Monday **to** Wednesday.	98, 99
Verb + Preposition	Everyone laughed **at** his joke.	100
Verb Forms after Prepositions	Carla is nervous about **taking** the exam.	101
Adjective + Preposition	I'm good **at** tennis.	102
Verb Complements	I am interested in **renting** a room.	103
Separable Two-Word Verbs	Do you want me to **type** it **up** today?	104

Answers to Exercises 105

Introduction

Many teachers believe that students acquire and retain a new language more rapidly and more efficiently when the structure and vocabulary of the language are presented in contexts; that is, when elements of a lesson such as grammar and lexicon are tied together in a real and meaningful setting. Exercises which do this—present material in a situational context—are referred to as contextualized exercises.

GrammarWork is a series of four contextualized exercise books for students of written English. These books may be used as major text or supplementary material, depending on whether a course is non-intensive or intensive, with any notional-functional or grammar-oriented syllabus. Each exercise presents vocabulary relating to a particular context and structures that are appropriate to that context together as a unit, rather than as isolated language fragments.

Book One is intended for the beginner: the student enrolled in a first-level English course with some exposure to the language. Book Two continues with beginners' material, proceeding from first-level to second-level work. Book Three is designed for the intermediate student, and Book Four is essentially a review of the first three books, adding occasional new material appropriate to intermediate levels. Book Four, particularly, was designed for both the native and the non-native student of English.

The exercises in each book are, for the most part, divided into three sections: 1) An examination of the structure to be presented ("Grammar"); 2) Exercises which enable the student to manipulate that new structure in a contextual setting ("Practice"); 3) A culminating exercise activity in which the student uses the material in the exercise by applying it to a personal, real-life situation ("Make It Work").

The Grammar section shows the student how to use the structure to be practiced, with diagrams and arrows that should be self-explanatory. Notes of explanation are supplied only when the grammar rule cannot be illustrated sufficiently.

Closely related to the *GrammarWork* exercises is an extensive grammar reference work, *GrammarGuide* by Janet Bing. This book explains and illustrates with examples the *GrammarWork* exercise items. The numbers at the beginning of each Grammar section in *GrammarWork* are coordinated with the *GrammarGuide* reference. For example, the number 2.13 under the heading Possessive of Nouns in the workbook indicates that a more comprehensive grammatical explanation of noun possessives is to be found in Chapter 2, item 13 of the reference book.

The Practice section consists of the contextualized exercises, usually a page in length and always self-contained; if a context is three pages instead of one, it will be self-contained within those three pages. Thus the teacher can select any exercise or group of exercises considered appropriate for a particular class or lesson and can also feel free to use only those exercises considered useful at a given time.

However, the teacher can also choose to utilize all the exercises in the order presented; the exercises have been written and arranged in ascending order of difficulty, with structures generally considered to be the easiest for most students to learn presented first.

The exercises are "self-contained" in that they have been designed for written practice without necessarily being preceded by an introductory teachers' presentation. Since grammatical explanations have been included and the new vocabulary is usually illustrated or defined, students can work independently, either at home or in class—in pairs or as a group. When students work together in pairs or in groups in the classroom, they should be encouraged to help each other; the teacher, too, can assist by circulating from pair to pair or group to group, guiding and correcting.

The Make It Work section enables students to apply what they have been practicing to freer, sometimes more natural situations. The activity usually contains a picture cue, a fill-in dialogue, or questions to answer. The purpose of Make it Work is to have the student experience the material in as close to a real-life setting as possible.

The perforated answer key can be used by either the student or the teacher. The teacher may choose to withhold the answers on some occasions; on other occasions, the students may be permitted to have access to the answer key for self-correcting purposes.

Acknowledgments

No book of this kind can be written without a great deal of help, at every step of the way, from both colleagues and friends. In particular, I would like to thank:

Gary Gabriel, my former teacher at Teachers College, Columbia University, whose help and encouragement brought me into the field of E.S.L. in New York and whose ideas have guided the philosophy behind this series.

Ken Sheppard, LaGuardia Community College; Ann Raimes, Hunter College; Darlene Larson, New York University; and David Tillyer and Karen Davy, my editors, for sharing ideas which have helped to shape these books.

Gloria Gallingane, LaGuardia Community College, and Janet Bing for their suggestions and support during the writing of these books.

P.B.

Irises and pansies are flowers.

Flowers

a daisy

a rose

an iris

a lily

an orchid

a pansy

Fruits

an apple

a peach

a strawberry

a cherry

a plum

a raspberry

Vegetables

a radish

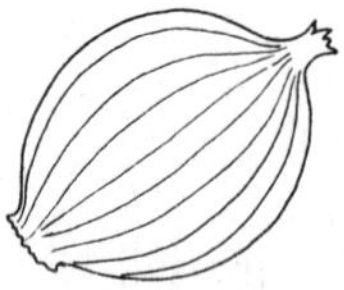

an onion

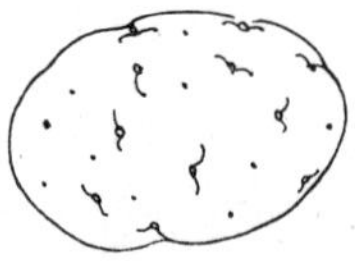

a potato

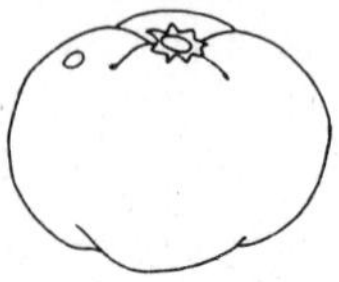

a tomato

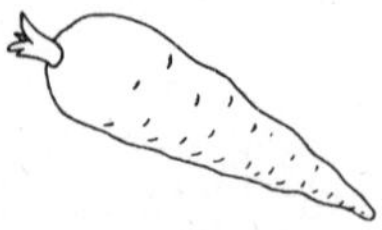

a carrot

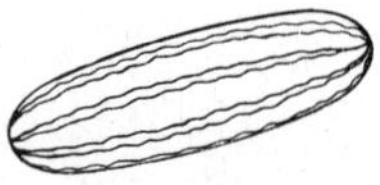

a cucumber

Irises and pansies are flowers.

REGULAR NOUN PLURALS: *-S, -ES, -IES*

GrammarGuide **2.3**

	-s	-es	-ies
	orchid-orchid s	peach-peach es	pansy-pans ies
	onion-onion s	tomato-tomato es	cherry-cherr ies
Note:	Add *-s* to form the plural.	Add *-es* to form the plural of words ending in *-s, -sh, -ch, -x, or -z.* Add *-es* to words ending in consonant + *o.*	Drop the *y* and add *-ies* to words ending in consonant + *y.*

Practice

Combine the sentences to form plurals.

1. A daisy is a flower.
   A rose is a flower. — Daisies and roses are flowers.
2. A radish is a vegetable.
   An onion is a vegetable. ____________________
3. A strawberry is a fruit.
   A raspberry is a fruit. ____________________
4. A potato is a vegetable.
   A carrot is a vegetable. ____________________
5. An iris is a flower.
   A pansy is a flower. ____________________
6. An apple is a fruit.
   A cherry is a fruit. ____________________
7. A lily is a flower.
   An orchid is a flower. ____________________
8. A cucumber is a vegetable.
   A tomato is a vegetable. ____________________
9. A plum is a fruit.
   A peach is a fruit. ____________________

Make It Work

Name two flowers you like. ____________________

Name two vegetables you like. ____________________

It's on a wooded lot with trees all around it.

-S VS. NO *-S* WITH COUNTABLE NOUNS
SIMPLE PRESENT

GrammarGuide
2.3

Singular	Plural	
a tree	**trees**	**a few trees**
one tree	**two trees**	**many trees**
	several trees	**all of the trees**

Practice

Fill in the blanks with the singular or plural form of the noun.

Gilbert: My wife and I just bought a new ___house___ (1. house).

David: What's it like?

Gilbert: It's on a wooded ________ (2. lot) with ________ (3. tree) all around it.

David: Is it one ________ (4. story) or two?

Gilbert: Two ________ (5. story). It has four ________ (6. room) on the first floor and three on the second floor.

David: Is it in good condition?

Gilbert: There are a few ________ (7. thing) that need to be done. Several ________ (8. room) need to be painted.

David: Well, that's easy to do. Is the kitchen modern?

Gilbert: Yes. It has a ________ (9. dishwasher), and all of the ________ (10. cabinet) are new.

David: How many ________ (11. bathroom) does it have?

Gilbert: Two and a half. It has a half ________ (12. bath) downstairs and two ________ (13. bath) upstairs.

David: It sounds great. When do you move in?

Gilbert: In about two ________ (14. month).

David: Congratulations and good luck in your new house.

New Word:
lot–an area of land used for one purpose

Could they be Doris Gross' keys?

POSSESSIVE OF NOUNS
QUESTIONS WITH *COULD*

GrammarGuide
2.13
5.7

Singular Form	Plural Form	Possessive Form
Doris		Dori s'
Gary		Gary 's
Gary's friend		Gary's friend 's
	the Dunns	the Dunn s'
	Gary's guests	Gary's guest s'

Note: Add -'s to form the possessive. If a noun ends in -s, add '.

Practice

Someone left his or her keys at Miriam's party by mistake. Whose could they be? Here's a list of everyone at the party. Make questions about the people on the list.

1. the Petersons — Could they be the Petersons'?
2. Susan Abbott — ______
3. David Barnes — ______
4. David's girlfriend — ______
5. the Kotches — ______
6. Susie Kirby — ______
7. Doris Gross — ______
8. Harry Schwartz — ______
9. Harry's friends — ______
10. Alex Dunn — ______
11. the Davises — ______
12. Jack Davis' brother — ______

Make It Work

Name three of your friends who might have left something at a party you gave. Then ask a question using *could*.

Becky Myers — Could that sweater be Becky Myers'?

______ ______

______ ______

______ ______

Antiques and Architecture

COUNTABLE AND UNCOUNTABLE NOUNS

GrammarGuide **2.4**

Uncountable Nouns	**Countable Nouns**
art	**games**
engineering	**biographies**
golf	
tennis	

Note: Add *-s* to countable nouns. Don't add *-s* to uncountable nouns. Fields of study and sports are usually uncountable.

Practice

Make the countable nouns plural.

Bargain Book Company offers readers a large selection of books in the following categories:

1.	antique	antiques
2.	architecture	—
3.	art	______
4.	baseball	______
5.	best-seller	______
6.	biography	______
7.	chemistry	______
8.	cooking	______
9.	dictionary	______
10.	engineering	______
11.	English	______
12.	history	______
13.	hobby	______
14.	indoor game	______
15.	Japanese	______
16.	music	______
17.	mystery	______
18.	pet	______
19.	philosophy	______
20.	tennis	______

Make It Work

Name three categories you're interested in.

______

______

______

New Words:
best-seller–a book that sells in large numbers
biography–the story of a person's life

I'd like more friends.
I'd like fewer acquaintances.

NOUN COMPARISONS WITH *MORE*, *LESS*, AND *FEWER*

GrammarGuide
2.21

I'd like [more] friends. I'd like [fewer] acquaintances.
I'd like [more] fun. I'd like [less] work.

Note: Use *more* with countable and uncountable nouns.
Use *less* with uncountable nouns; use *fewer* with countable nouns.

Practice

Tell if you would like *more, less,* or *fewer* of the following things in your life. Fill in the blanks.

1. I'd like ___more___ fun.
2. I'd like ___less___ work.
3. I'd like __________ time to myself.
4. I'd like __________ love.
5. I'd like __________ problems.
6. I'd like __________ happiness.
7. I'd like __________ sadness.
8. I'd like __________ arguments.
9. I'd like __________ money.
10. I'd like __________ pressure.
11. I'd like __________ encouragement.
12. I'd like __________ criticism.
13. I'd like __________ advice.
14. I'd like __________ friends.
15. I'd like __________ acquaintances.

Make It Work

Name one thing you would like more of. ______________________________

Name one thing you would like less of. ______________________________

New Words:
encouragement–giving hope or courage to someone
criticism–giving an unfavorable opinion
advice–the opinion given by one person to another telling the other how he or she should act

New City has the fewest schools of the three.

	New City	Midland	Bridgetown
 **Population**	1,867,760	1,453,343	1,652,794
 **Schools**	201	311	284
 **Fire Fighters**	1,846	762	1,287
 **Police Officers**	3,935	2,503	3,125
 **Criminal Offenses**	218,571	50,649	111,935

New City has the fewest schools of the three.

NOUN COMPARISONS WITH *LESS, THE LEAST, FEWER,* AND *THE FEWEST*

SIMPLE PRESENT

GrammarGuide
2.21

New City has [fewer] schools than Bridgetown.

New City has [the fewest] schools of the three cities.

Midland has [less] crime than Bridgetown.

Midland has [the least] crime of the three.

Note: Use *fewer* and *the fewest* with countable nouns. Use *less* and *the least* with uncountable nouns. *More* and *the most* are used with both countable and uncountable nouns.

When *crime* is a general category, it is uncountable. When it is an individual act, it is countable.

Practice

Look at the chart on page 6. Then compare the three cities. Fill in the blanks with *less, fewer, more, the least, the fewest,* or *the most.*

1. Bridgetown has _____ fewer _____ people than New City.
2. New City has _____ the most _____ people of the three cities.
3. New City has ______________ schools of the three.
4. Midland has ______________ schools of the three.
5. Midland has ______________ fire fighters of the three.
6. Bridgetown has ______________ fire fighters than New City.
7. New City has ______________ fire fighters of the three.
8. Midland has ______________ police officers of the three.
9. Bridgetown has ______________ police officers than Midland.
10. Bridgetown has ______________ police officers than New City.
11. Midland has ______________ crime than Bridgetown.
12. By far, Midland has ______________ crime of the three.
13. Bridgetown has ______________ crime than New City.
14. New City has ______________ crime of the three.
15. And yet, New City has ______________ police officers of the three.

Make It Work

Name two reasons to live in Midland.

Midland has ____

____

____

A university library

A VS. *AN*

GrammarGuide **2.6**

a delicatessen	**an attorney**
a furniture store	**an exterminator**
a yarn shop	**an X-ray technician**
	an interior decorator
	an optician
a hobby shop, but →	**an honest insurance agent**
a university library, but →	**an unusual interior decorator**

Note: Use *an* before vowel sounds; use *a* before all other sounds.

Practice

Angela just moved into a new house. She's new in the area and she needs to know where she can find the following stores and services.

Fill in the blanks with *a* or *an*.

1. __a__ hairdresser
2. _____ attorney
3. _____ plumber
4. _____ licensed electrician
5. _____ interior decorator
6. _____ qualified veterinarian
7. _____ insurance agent
8. _____ automobile mechanic
9. _____ reliable baby-sitter
10. _____ honest tax accountant
11. _____ optician
12. _____ dentist
13. _____ experienced painter
14. _____ dependable gardener
15. _____ exterminator
16. _____ locksmith
17. _____ good dry cleaner
18. _____ hospital
19. _____ X-ray laboratory
20. _____ animal hospital
21. _____ university library
22. _____ employment agency
23. _____ United Bank
24. _____ yarn shop
25. _____ unusual gift shop
26. _____ inexpensive restaurant
27. _____ uniform rental company
28. _____ hardware store
29. _____ appliance center
30. _____ health food store

New Words:
optician–a person who makes and sells eyeglasses
exterminator–a person who kills unwanted animals and insects
locksmith–a person who makes and repairs locks
yarn–a thread made of wool

Are you a licensed electrician?

A AND *AN* BEFORE ADJECTIVES
SIMPLE PRESENT

GrammarGuide **2.6**

Are you [an] electrician?

Are you [a] licensed electrician?

Note: Put *a* or *an* before adjectives followed by countable nouns.

Practice

Below are some listings in the telephone directory. Ask each person or institution a question using the word in parentheses.

1. D. V. Dowl, Electrician (licensed) Are you a licensed electrician?
2. A. J. Edwards, Plumber (registered) ____________
3. Lester Cole, Ford Dealer (authorized) ____________
4. Barbara Schwartz, Pharmacist (licensed) ____________
5. S. Y. Kong, Nurse (registered) ____________
6. L. W. McKay, Public Accountant (certified) ____________
7. Century Savings Bank (insured) ____________
8. Oakdale Day Care Center (licensed) ____________
9. Evans Computer School (accredited) ____________
10. Dave's Boat Company Evinrude Dealer (authorized) ____________

New Words:
registered, licensed–having official permission to practice a profession or run a business
certified–having a document stating you have completed requirements for a profession
accredited–meeting official or state requirements
authorized–having permission to sell or repair certain products

Snow melts. An ice cube melts.

NO ARTICLE VS. *A* AND *AN*
COUNTABLE AND UNCOUNTABLE NOUNS

GrammarGuide
2.8

Name something that melts. [   ] **snow**
[**an**] **ice cube**

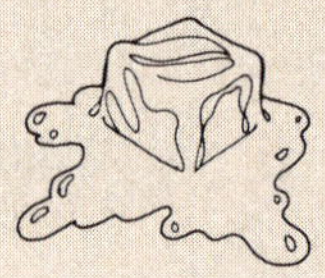

Note: Use *a* or *an* with singular countable nouns.
Don't use *a* or *an* with uncountable nouns.

Practice

Give two answers for each statement. Write only **singular** words.

Name two things that melt.	1. ice cream 2. an ice cube
Name two things you polish.	3. ____ 4. ____
Name two things you button.	5. ____ 6. ____
Name two things you tie.	7. ____ 8. ____
Name two things you eat by the slice.	9. ____ 10. ____
Name two things that are delivered every day.	11. ____ 12. ____
Name two fruits you can eat without peeling.	13. ____ 14. ____
Name two things you buy by the gallon.	15. ____ 16. ____
Name two large animals.	17. ____ 18. ____
Name two necessary machines in an office.	19. ____ 20. ____

New Word:
peel–remove the outer covering

She walked into the bathroom and grabbed a toothbrush.

A* VS. *THE

SIMPLE PAST

GrammarGuide **2.7**

She looked up at [the] sky. [The] sun wasn't shining.

She grabbed [an] umbrella and left [the] house.

Note: Use *the* when you refer to only one of something:
the sky the sun the moon

Use *the* for things at home or in the community when people know which one you are talking about:
the car the train station

Use *a* or *an* for unspecified objects:
an umbrella a sweater

Do not use *a* or *an* with plural or uncountable nouns:
clothes weather

Practice

Fill in the blanks with *a* or *the*.

1. She got __a__ suitcase from __the__ bedroom closet.
2. Then she put ____ pair of jeans and ____ T-shirt into the suitcase.
3. She went into ____ bathroom and looked into ____ medicine cabinet.
4. She grabbed ____ bottle of aspirin and ____ toothbrush.
5. Then she walked downstairs and watered ____ plants.
6. She closed ____ windows and pulled down ____ shades.
7. She locked ____ door and left ____ house.
8. As she was getting into ____ car, she looked up at ____ black clouds in ____ sky.
9. She hoped that ____ weather would be good.
10. She got into ____ car and drove to ____ airport.

Make It Work

Answer the questions.

Where do you keep your umbrella? I keep it on a hook in the downstairs closet.

Where do you keep your suitcase? ________

Where do you keep your clothes? ________

New Word:
grab–take with a sudden movement

Shirts were half price. I bought a shirt.

NO ARTICLE VS. *A* OR *THE*

SIMPLE PRESENT, PRESENT CONTINUOUS, SIMPLE PAST, FUTURE WITH *WILL*

GrammarGuide
2.7
2.9

[ ] Shirts were half price.	**[ ] Shirts were half price.**
I bought [a] shirt for my husband.	**I bought two shirts for my husband.**
[The] shirt cost $8.50.	**[The] shirts were $8.50 each.**

Note: **Do not use an article for general statements.**

Use *a* and *an* for a single unspecified object, especially when mentioning it for the first time.

Use *the* for a particular object, especially when it is followed by a modifier or when it has been mentioned before.

Practice

Fill in the blanks with *a* (or *an*), *the*, or a line for nothing (---).

1. Smith's Farm Market is __an__ outdoor market.
2. It sells everything from ____ antiques to fresh vegetables.
3. ____ market opens at 7:00 on Tuesdays and stays open all day.
4. But you have to be there early if you want to get ____ parking space.
5. By about 8:00, Smith's Market is packed with ____ people.
6. If you are looking for ____ vegetables, you'll find top quality and unbeatable prices.

Shirts were half price. I bought a shirt.

7. Last week, for instance, I bought ____ entire basket of tomatoes for only 50¢.

8. ____ mushrooms I bought were only $1.00 a pound.

9. You'll also get good buys on ____ household goods like ____ mops and ____ brooms or even ____ sheets and ____ towels.

10. I bought ____ sheet and ____ two towels for the total price of $12.00.

11. ____ sheet was $6.00 and ____ towels were $3.00 each.

12. At any department store, ____ sheets sell for about $12.00 each.

13. You can also buy ____ clothes at Smith's Market.

14. I bought ____ beautiful wool sweater there.

15. ____ sweater cost $13.95.

16. There were items like ____ watches for sale.

17. ____ watches they were selling were name brands like Timex and Bulova.

18. I bought ____ watch for only $6.00.

19. I also saw ____ rug for $15.00. Now I'm sorry I didn't buy it.

20. Next week I'm going back to Smith's Market, and if ____ rug is still there, I'll buy it.

Make It Work

Tell about the last time you went to a sale.

I went to a fantastic sale at ____ .
______________________________ on sale. I bought ______________________________________ .
______________ cost only ______________ . I also ______________________________________
____
____ .

I'm going to buy a broom and some kitchen towels.

A VS. *SOME*

GrammarGuide
2.7

The next time I go to Smith's Farm Market,

I'm going to buy [a] broom and [some] kitchen towels.

Note: Use *a* with singular countable nouns.

Use *some* with plural countable nouns or uncountable nouns.

Sometimes it is possible to omit *some*, but not *a* or *an*.

Practice

This is what I plan to buy at Smith's Market next week.

Fill in the blanks with *a* (or *an*) or *some*.

1. __some__ fresh ham
2. ________ homemade cookies
3. ________ loaf of freshly baked bread
4. ________ tomatoes
5. ________ plant
6. ________ dried flowers
7. ________ hammer
8. ________ nails
9. ________ steak knives
10. ________ pair of scissors
11. ________ stationery
12. ________ antique jewelry
13. ________ leather wallet
14. ________ antique lamp
15. ________ gifts for the holidays

Make It Work

List five things that you need to buy. Use *a* (or *an*) and *some*.

____

____

____

____

____

He'll go to school in the fall.

NO ARTICLE VS. *THE* WITH EXPRESSIONS OF TIME AND PLACE

SIMPLE PRESENT, SIMPLE PAST, FUTURE WITH *WILL*

GrammarGuide **2.9**

Expressions with *the*	Expressions without *the*
[the] beginning, [the] end	at [ ] first
[the] past, [the] present	
in [the] evening	at [ ] noon
in [the] spring	at [ ] night
[the] 23rd of January	[ ] January 23rd
go to [the] university	go to [ ] school
go to [the] bookstore	go to [ ] church
	go [ ] home

Practice

Fill in the blanks with *the* or a line for nothing (---).

1. Kosho plans to go to --- college --- next year.
2. He'll go to _____ school in _____ fall.
3. The first semester begins on _____ September 15th and lasts until _____ middle of January.
4. The second semester begins at _____ end of January and continues until _____ 20th of May.
5. At _____ first Kosho will be very busy getting used to his new schedule.
6. His courses begin at 8:00 in _____ morning and last until _____ noon.
7. At _____ noon he'll go to _____ cafeteria and eat a quick lunch.
8. Then he'll go to _____ work.
9. He has a part-time job in _____ afternoon.
10. He'll work until 5:00 in _____ evening.
11. Then he'll go _____ home and study.
12. He's worried about _____ future. He doesn't know if he can handle a job and his schoolwork.

Make It Work

Tell about your English course. Fill in the blanks.

It started in _______________ (season). It began on _______________

and lasts until _______________. It meets on _______________

at _______________ in _______________.

A trip to the Metropolitan Museum and Central Park

GrammarGuide
2.9

	place names without *the*	place names with *the*
continents	North America South America	
countries	Canada	the United States
points of the compass	northern New York	the North
cities and states	Bogotá New York	
bodies of water: rivers, oceans, seas, lakes, bays	Lake Ontario	the Atlantic Ocean
mountain ranges		the Catskill Mountains (the Catskills)
single mountains	Whiteface Mountain	
islands	Coney Island	
hotels		the Hilton Hotel
parks	Central Park	
museums and libraries		the Museum of Modern Art the New York Public Library
streets	Forty-second Street Madison Avenue	the Avenue of the Americas
colleges and universities	New York University	the City University of New York

A trip to the Metropolitan Museum and Central Park

NO ARTICLE VS. *THE* WITH PLACE NAMES

Practice

Look at page 16. Then fill in the blanks with *the* or a line for no article (---).

New York! Now Only $799!

1. ▶ one week in _the_ United States
2. ▶ round-trip airfare from _---_ South America to _---_ New York
3. ▶ room with a private bath at ____ Sheridan Hotel, conveniently located on ____ Park Avenue

▶ expert tour guides with a full program of tours

4. • a boat trip of ____ New York on ____ Hudson River
5. • a tour to ____ Liberty Island and the Statue of Liberty
6. • a bus tour down ____ Fifth Avenue to ____ Wall Street with a stop at the World Trade Center
7. • a visit to two famous universities, ____ City University of New York and ____ Columbia University
8. • a trip to ____ New York Public Library and ____ Metropolitan Museum
9. • a visit to ____ Central Park

For an Additional $400

10. ▶ travel to ____ Lake Placid, located in ____ northern New York State
11. • see the place where the 1980 Winter Olympics were held in ____ Adirondack Mountains
12. • visit ____ Mount Marcy, the highest point in New York State

Or

13. ▶ travel to ____ Lake Ontario to the world-famous Niagara Falls
14. • visit ____ Canada, which is only minutes away

15. Departures every Tuesday from ____ Bogotá or ____ Caracas.

For more information, call
Northern Airlines
(212) 555-1100

Make It Work

Name two things you would like to see in New York.

______________________ ______________________

Madeleine painted the entire kitchen herself.

REFLEXIVE PRONOUNS

SIMPLE PRESENT, SIMPLE PAST, FUTURE WITH *WILL*

GrammarGuide **3.8**

Singular			Plural		
I did	**it**	**myself.**	**We did**	**it**	**ourselves.**
You did	**it**	**yourself.**	**You did**	**it**	**yourselves.**
He did	**it**	**himself.**	**They did**	**it**	**themselves.**
She did	**it**	**herself.**			

Note: Reflexive pronouns refer back to the subject.
Note that singular reflexives end in *-self*. Plural reflexives end in *-selves*.

Practice

Fill in the blanks with a reflexive pronoun.

Madeleine and Garret bought an old house in Missouri. After they moved in, they discovered that the kitchen needed a lot of work. They didn't have much money, so they decided to do most of the work themselves (1.).

When they first decided to redo the kitchen, people told them that they could never do it ________ (2.). "But," said Madeleine, "we read lots of do-it-yourself books and magazines, and then we began. Slowly, we learned to do everything ________ (3.)."

First, they removed the old kitchen cabinets and counters. Then Garret put in new cabinets, which he built ________ (4.). "I didn't think I could build those cabinets," Garret said, "but once I started, I realized that I could do all of the work ________ (5.). It's much cheaper if you do it ________ (6.), and you can save ________ (7.) thousands of dollars."

Madeleine painted the entire kitchen ________ (8.). The kitchen table looked old and ugly until Madeleine refinished it. She even made the place mats on the table ________ (9.). "Really, I enjoyed doing it ________ (10.)," said Madeleine. "It's also a nice feeling to know you can make something ________ (11.). Next year we hope to add a family room to the house. Of course, we'll do all of the work ________ (12.)."

New Words:
redo–do again
remove–take away
refinish–put a new surface on

The others are tall.

ANOTHER, THE OTHER, AND *THE OTHERS*

SIMPLE PRESENT, PRESENT CONTINUOUS

GrammarGuide
3.9

One woman is short.	**The others**	**are tall.**
Four women are tall.	**The other**	**is short.**
Three women are wearing dresses.	**Another**	**is wearing a suit.**

Note: ***the others*** **= the only ones left (plural)**
the other **= the only one left (singular)**
another **= one of several (singular)**

Practice

Fill in the blanks with *another, the other,* or *the others.*

One woman is short.
1. The others are tall.

Four women are thin.
2. ______________ is fat.

One woman is fat.
3. ______________ are thin.

Four women are middle-aged.
4. ______________ is young.

Three women are wearing dresses.
5. ______________ is wearing a suit.

6. ______________ is wearing pants.

Four women have short hair.
7. ______________ has long hair.

One woman has a hat on.
8. ______________ don't have hats on.

Two women have high heels on.
9. ______________ has boots on.

One woman isn't smiling.
10. ______________ are smiling.

Someone broke into his apartment.

INDEFINITE PRONOUNS

SIMPLE PAST

GrammarGuide **3.9**

Someone broke into his apartment.

Nothing was missing.

There wasn't **anything** broken.

Note: **Use *someone* (or *somebody*) for people and *something* for things.**
***Some* and *no* are used with positive verbs; *any* is used with negative verbs.**
***No one* is two words. All other indefinite pronouns are one word.**

Practice

Fill in the blanks with *someone, something, anyone, anything, no one,* or *nothing*. Read the entire sentence first.

1. When Jack got home, it was very late at night. The street was deserted. <u>No one</u> was around.
2. He walked into his apartment building. There were no people in the lobby. He didn't see __________ in the halls, either.
3. The door of his apartment was open, but __________ was there.
4. The lock on his door was damaged, but __________ else in the apartment was broken.
5. He looked around the apartment. Fortunately, he discovered that __________ of value was missing.
6. He called the police, and they sent __________ over right away.
7. He explained that __________ had broken into his apartment.
8. A police officer looked around the apartment building for the robber, but she didn't find __________ .
9. She told Jack to have __________ put a new lock on his door immediately.
10. There wasn't __________ else the police officer could do for him, so she left.

Make It Work

Fill in the blanks with the correct indefinite pronoun.

POLICE REPORT

Sept. 23, __________

Apartment 2B at 566 East Worth Street was broken into. Apparently __________ entered the premises between the hours of 8:00 p.m. and 1:00 a.m. A routine investigation was made. __________ was hurt. __________ appeared to be missing from the premises. __________ was arrested.

Whose jewelry was stolen?

WHO'S* VS. *WHOSE

SIMPLE PRESENT, PRESENT CONTINUOUS, SIMPLE PAST

GrammarGuide
3.7

Whose **jewelry was stolen?**

Who's **a suspect in the robbery?**

Note: ***Whose* shows possession.**
***Who's* is a contraction for *who is*.**

Practice

An hour ago, a house in a wealthy suburb was robbed. The person who lives in the house is missing, and so is all of the money in the safe. Some jewelry, including a diamond ring, is also missing.

Fill in the blanks with *whose* or *who's*.

1. ___Whose___ house was robbed?
2. __________ the owner of the house?
3. __________ missing?
4. Was the person __________ house was robbed home at the time?
5. __________ money was stolen?
6. __________ jewelry was in the safe?
7. __________ diamond ring was it?
8. __________ a suspect in the robbery?
9. Is the person __________ missing a suspect?
10. __________ fingerprints are on the safe?
11. __________ investigating the robbery?
12. __________ the robber?

Make It Work

You are a police officer investigating the robbery. Ask three important questions.

____

____

____

New Words:
safe–a metal box with a lock used to protect valuable things from robbers and fire
suspect–a person who is believed to be guilty
fingerprint–the mark of a finger, especially used in solving crimes
investigate–examine the reasons for something
suburb–the outer area of a city

There are no lights on. They're not at home.

THEY'RE, THERE, AND THE POSSESSIVE ADJECTIVE *THEIR*
SIMPLE PRESENT, PRESENT CONTINUOUS, SIMPLE PAST

GrammarGuide
3.4

There	**are no lights on.**
Their	**porch light isn't on, either.**
They're	**not at home.**

Note: ***There* often replaces the subject. It is usually followed by the verb *to be* in statements or preceded by the verb *to be* in questions.**
***Their* shows possession.**
***They're* is a contraction for *they are*.**

Practice

Fill in the blanks with *there, their,* or *they're.*

Linda: There (1.) are no lights on. ____________ (2.) not at home.

Fred: What? ____________ (3.) expecting us for dinner! Are you sure this is ____________ (4.) house?

Linda: Yes, of course. ____________ (5.) house is tan, and ____________ (6.) are big trees in the front yard.

Fred: I don't think this is ____________ (7.) house. Isn't ____________ (8.) a fence in the front?

Linda: Maybe ____________ (9.) is.

Fred: What's ____________ (10.) address?

Linda: 2562 Mountainview Road.

Fred: ____________ (11.) must be a mistake. This is 2562, but this isn't ____________ (12.) house. Are you sure we're on the right street?

Linda: I'm not positive. It's dark, and ____________ (13.) are no street lights.

Fred: Didn't the street sign say Mountain Road?

Linda: Yes.

Fred: What's the name of ____________ (14.) street again?

Linda: Mountainview.

Fred: No wonder ____________ (15.) not at home. This is the wrong street.

Heat costs me $65.70 a month.

SUBJECT-VERB AGREEMENT

SIMPLE PRESENT

GrammarGuide **4.4**

Rent **costs** **me $425.00 a month.**

Mortgage payments **cost** **me $327.98 a month.**

Note: Use singular verb forms with uncountable nouns:

rent	**heat**	**food**	**medicine**
water	**gas**	**electricity**	**entertainment**

Practice

Below is a list of monthly expenses. Write the amount (in dollars, lire, pesos, etc.) you spend for each item every month. Fill in as many items as you can. Use *cost* or *costs*.

1. mortgage payments Mortgage payments cost me $327.98 a month.
2. heat Heat costs me $65.70 a month.
3. rent ______
4. gas ______
5. electricity ______
6. water ______
7. car payments ______
8. gas for the car ______
9. food ______
10. medicine ______
11. haircuts ______
12. dry cleaning ______
13. telephone bills ______
14. clothes ______
15. entertainment ______

New Word:

mortgage–an agreement to borrow money, especially on a house or land; the house belongs to the lender until the money is paid back

My husband and I clean the house.

SUBJECT-VERB AGREEMENT
SIMPLE PRESENT

GrammarGuide
4.4
1.14

Who cleans the house in your family?

My mother **My wife** **My husband** **A cleaning woman**	**cleans**	**the house.**
My husband and I **I**	**clean**	**the house.**

Practice

Answer the questions with long answers.

1. Who fixes breakfast in your family? My husband fixes breakfast.
2. Who pays the bills? __________
3. Who takes out the trash? __________
4. Who buys birthday and holiday gifts? __________
5. Who fixes broken items around the house? __________
6. Who cleans the house? __________
7. Who shines your shoes? __________
8. Who sews on your buttons? __________
9. Who cuts your hair? __________
10. Who washes your clothes? __________

Make It Work

Name three household chores and tell who does them in your family.

I do the errands.

MAKE VS. *DO*

SIMPLE PRESENT

GrammarGuide
6.8

Use *do* with these expressions:	Use *make* with these expressions:
my homework	breakfast, lunch, dinner
an assignment	dessert
the housework	the beds
the yardwork	an appointment
the dishes	plans
the laundry	arrangements
the ironing	a telephone call
the shopping	an effort
the errands	
the typing	
the correspondence	

Practice

Below is a list of chores. Tell who does each chore in your family. Use *make* or *do* and the present tense.

1. the laundry — I do the laundry.
2. the ironing ____________
3. dinner ____________
4. the dinner dishes ____________
5. the food shopping ____________
6. the bed (beds) ____________
7. doctor appointments ____________
8. the housework ____________
9. plans to see friends ____________
10. the correspondence ____________
11. travel arrangements ____________
12. the errands ____________
13. hotel and restaurant reservations ____________
14. the typing ____________
15. the yardwork ____________

New Word:
correspondence–the writing and exchanging of letters

She doesn't make a lot of money, but she works very hard.

SIMPLE FORM VS. PRESENT FORM

GrammarGuide
4.2
4.4

Sometimes she [gets] a part in a play.
Sometimes she doesn't [get] a part in a play.

Practice

Fill in the blanks with the correct form of the verb in parentheses.

Katie West is an actress. She doesn't __make__ (1. make) a lot of money, but she ______ (2. work) very hard. She ______ (3. take) voice lessons every morning, and in the afternoon she ______ (4. study) acting. She's sometimes so busy that she doesn't ______ (5. have) time for lunch.

Once or twice a week, she ______ (6. have) an audition. When she ______ (7. go) to an audition, she doesn't always ______ (8. get) a part in a play. Sometimes she ______ (9. get) a part in a television commercial. A television commercial only ______ (10. last) for a minute, but Katie ______ (11. practice) her part for hours. Being an actress is a lot of hard work, but Katie ______ (12. love) it.

Make It Work

Tell about your present job (at work or at home).

I ______________________. I ______________________.

I don't always ______________________. ______________________
______________________.

New Words:
audition–a test performance by an actor or actress
part–a character acted by an actor or actress

There are excellent cultural events in a big city.

SUBJECT-VERB AGREEMENT WITH *THERE IS* AND *THERE ARE*

GrammarGuide
3.5
1.14

There | **are** | **a lot of well-paying jobs in a big city.**

There | **'s** | **a great deal of crime in a big city.**

Note: ***There is*** **(or** ***there are*****) agrees with the subject that follows it.**

Use ***there are*** **with plural nouns; use** ***there is*** **with uncountable nouns:**
industry crime pollution litter noise

Practice

Fill in the blanks with *there's* or *there are.*

1. There are several good reasons to live in a big city.
2. ______________ a lot of industry in a big city.
3. ______________ a lot of well-paying jobs available.
4. ______________ excellent cultural events in a big city.
5. ______________ all kinds of movies, plays, and concerts.
6. ______________ a lot of shops in a big city.
7. ______________ small specialty shops and large department stores.
8. ______________ some good reasons *not* to live in a big city.
9. ______________ a great deal of crime.
10. ______________ a lot of robberies every day.
11. ______________ a lot of pollution in a big city.
12. ______________ air pollution from factories.
13. ______________ also litter on the streets.
14. ______________ a lot of noise in a big city.
15. ______________ sirens, trucks, and cars at night and during the day.

Make It Work

Write a paragraph about living in a big city. Give three good reasons to live in a big city OR three good reasons not to live in a big city.

There are three good reasons ______________________________.
First, ______________________________. ______________________________
______________________________. Second, ______________________________
______________________________. Third, ______________________________
______________________________.
____

As he came in, he turned to Mr. Jones and said, "Bon appetit."

REGULAR AND IRREGULAR PAST TENSE VERBS

GrammarGuide
4.14
6.2

Regular Verbs

arrive – arrive [d]

turn – turn [ed]

Note: To form the past tense of regular verbs, add *-d* or *-ed* to the simple form of the verb.

Irregular Verbs

sit – sat
think – thought
come – came
say – said
know – knew
stand – stood
understand – understood
get – got
meet – met
tell – told

Practice

Fill in the blanks with the past tense of the verb in parentheses.

An American named Jones was on a boat trip. The first day of the trip, he ___sat___ (1. sit) opposite a Frenchman for lunch. The Frenchman ____________ (2. arrive) late. As

As he came in, he turned to Mr. Jones and said, "Bon appetit."

he __________ (3. come) in, he __________ (4. turn) to Mr. Jones and __________ (5. say), "Bon appetit." Mr. Jones, who __________ (6. know) no French at all, __________ (7. think) that the Frenchman was giving his name, so he __________ (8. stand) up and said, "Jones."

The second day, the Frenchman arrived late and said, "Bon appetit." Mr. Jones __________ (9. get) up and said, "Jones." The third day, the same thing __________ (10. happen).

The fourth day, as Mr. Jones was taking a morning walk around the boat, he __________ (11. meet) an old friend. His friend __________ (12. ask) him how the trip was going. Mr. Jones __________ (13. mention) that there was an Italian man named Bonappeti opposite him at lunch. His friend __________ (14. understand) the situation immediately. He __________ (15. explain) that the man wasn't Italian. He __________ (16. tell) Mr. Jones that the man was French and that he was wishing him a pleasant lunch. Mr. Jones __________ (17. decide) to correct the situation.

Mr. Jones arrived late for lunch that day. When he __________ (18. walk) into the dining area, the Frenchman was already eating. Mr. Jones __________ (19. say), "Bon appetit." The Frenchman __________ (20. smile) and said, "Jones."

Make It Work

Look at the picture on page 28. The conversation between Mr. Jones and the Frenchman is missing. Write the correct conversation on the picture. (Mr. Jones is standing.)

She wrote her first book at the age of 24.

REGULAR AND IRREGULAR PAST TENSE VERBS

GrammarGuide
4.14
6.2

Irregular Verbs

be – was/were	**become – became**
have – had	**grow – grew**
go – went	**read – read**
spend – spent	**write – wrote**

Practice

Fill in the blanks with the past tense of the verb in parentheses.

Agatha Christie, one of the most popular writers in the English language, was born in 1891 and died (1. die) in 1976. She __________ (2. grow) up in a small town in England. She never __________ (3. go) to school, but she __________ (4. read) a great deal when she was young. "I __________ (5. have) a very lazy childhood," she once __________ (6. say). "I __________ (7. spend) most of my time making up stories. It __________ (8. be) a very happy life."

Agatha Christie __________ (9. decide) to write her first book because she __________ (10. want) to prove to her sister that she could write a good mystery story. In 1915, at the age of 24, she __________ (11. write) *The Mysterious Affair at Styles.* Six publishers __________ (12. reject) the book, but it was finally published in 1920. After that, she ____________ (13. publish) one mystery story a year until her death.

Her private life ____________ (14. be) ordinary in contrast to her detective stories. She ____________ (15. think) of most of her ideas while she was doing chores around the house. "In fact," she once ____________ (16. say), "some of my best ideas ____________ (17. come) to me while working at the kitchen sink."

During her lifetime, Agatha Christie ____________ (18. write) more than 70 detective stories; 31 of her stories ____________ (19. become) plays or movies. But she ____________ (20. confess), "People think writing is easy for me. It isn't. It's murder."

New Words:
childhood–the time when someone is a child
reject–not accept
ordinary–not unusual
confess–admit something wrong, especially a crime
make up–invent

She didn't go to school.

SIMPLE FORM VS. PAST FORM

GrammarGuide
4.2
6.4
4.14

She didn't [go] to school.
Her mother [tutored] her.
As a child, she liked to [read].

Practice

Fill in the blanks with the simple form or the past tense of the verb in parentheses.

1. (grow) Agatha Christie didn't ___grow___ up in a large city.
2. (grow) She ____________ up in a small town in England.
3. (go) She didn't ____________ to school.
4. (tutor) Her mother ____________ her.
5. (read) Agatha Christie learned to ____________ when she was very young.
6. (make) She had a vivid imagination, and she liked to ____________ up stories.
7. (challenge) When she was in her twenties, Agatha's sister ____________ her to write a book.
8. (accept) Agatha agreed to ____________ the challenge.
9. (complete) She ____________ her first novel in 1915.
10. (publish) Since she was an unknown writer, most publishers didn't want to ____________ her novel.
11. (reject) Six publishers ____________ the book, but it was finally published five years later.
12. (have) After that, she ____________ no trouble getting her books published.
13. (have) Even though Agatha's novels are exciting, she didn't ____________ an especially exciting private life. In fact, her life was rather ordinary.
14. (think) People naturally ____________ writing was easy for Agatha because she wrote so many books.
15. (think) But Agatha didn't ____________ it was easy.

New Words:
tutor–teach by private instruction
vivid imagination–clear, lifelike pictures in the mind
challenge–invite someone to compete

I heard a funny joke yesterday.

IRREGULAR PAST TENSE VERBS

GrammarGuide **6.2**

buy–bought
bring–brought
send–sent
lend–lent
drink–drank
swim–swam
throw–threw
fly–flew
eat–ate
find–found
take–took
sleep–slept
ride–rode
wear–wore
hear–heard

When did you last hear a funny joke?

I [heard] a funny joke yesterday.
two days ago.
a month ago.

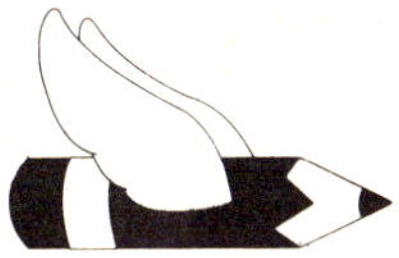

Practice

Answer the questions. Tell about yourself.

1. When did you last drink champagne? I drank champagne two months ago.
2. When did you last take a nap? ______
3. When did you last hear a funny joke? ______
4. When did you last lend someone money? ______
5. When did you last buy something on sale? ______
6. When did you last eat at a fancy restaurant? ______
7. When did you last send someone a post card? ______
8. When did you last wear something green? ______
9. When did you last sleep until noon? ______
10. When did you last ride a bicycle? ______
11. When did you last bring someone flowers? ______
12. When did you last throw a party? ______
13. When did you last swim in the ocean? ______
14. When did you last find money on the sidewalk? ______
15. When did you last fly on a jet? ______

New Expression:
throw a party–give a party

He'll fly to San Juan, Puerto Rico.

AFFIRMATIVE STATEMENTS
FUTURE WITH *GOING TO* AND *WILL*

GrammarGuide
4.7
4.8

He | **'s going to fly** | **to San Juan, Puerto Rico.**
He | **'ll fly** | **to San Juan, Puerto Rico.**

Note: ***Be going to*** **and *will* both express future time.**

Contractions: he's → he is
he'll → he will

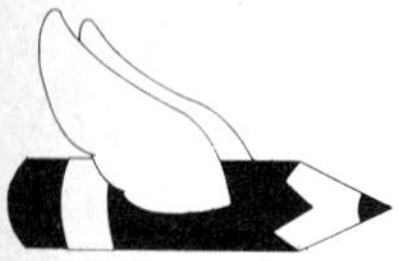

Practice

A Ten-Day Caribbean Cruise Aboard a Luxury Liner only $899–$1139!

A friend is going to take this cruise. Tell about his itinerary. For each item, make two sentences expressing future time. Use contractions whenever possible.

• Sail from Puerto Rico to St. Thomas on December 1.
1. He's going to sail from Puerto Rico to St. Thomas on December 1.
2. __________

• Stop in Antigua on December 3.
3. __________
4. __________

• Visit Martinique on December 5.
5. __________
6. __________

• See Trinidad on December 8.
7. __________
8. __________

• Stay in Caracas on December 9 and 10.
9. __________
10. __________

• Fly back to Puerto Rico on December 11.
11. __________
12. __________

New Word:
cruise–a trip on a boat

He'll do some shopping when he's in St. Thomas.

STATEMENTS WITH *BEFORE, AFTER, WHEN,* AND *AS SOON AS*
FUTURE WITH *WILL* AND *WON'T*

GrammarGuide
4.7
8.12

He 'll arrive in San Juan after he leaves New York.

After he leaves New York, he'll arrive in San Juan.

Note: To express a future idea, use the present tense in clauses beginning with *before, when, after,* and *as soon as.* Use the future tense in the main clause.

Practice

Victor is going to take a Caribbean cruise this winter. Read each sentence first. Then fill in the blanks with the correct verb tense. Use contractions whenever possible.

1. Victor ___will arrive___ (arrive) in San Juan after he ___leaves___ (leave) New York.
2. He ________ (go) to St. Thomas after he ________ (see) San Juan.
3. He ________ (do) some shopping when he ________ (be) in St. Thomas.
4. After he ________ (visit) St. Thomas, he ________ (go) to Martinique.
5. As soon as he ________ (arrive) there, he ________ (go) swimming.
6. He ________ (buy) some French perfume too.
7. He ________ (not/go) to Barbados after he ________ (leave) Martinique. The ship doesn't stop there.
8. Instead, he ________ (go) to La Guaira.
9. When he ________ (be) in La Guaira, he ________ (visit) the city of Caracas.
10. He wants to fly to Curacao on his own, but he probably ________ (not/have) time.

New Expression:
on his own–alone

One of the boys is sitting in two seats.

One of the boys is sitting in two seats.

SUBJECT-VERB AGREEMENT

PRESENT CONTINUOUS

The older man | **is sitting** | **down.**

The young woman and the older woman | **are standing** | **up.**

The woman with all the packages | **is sleeping.**

One of the teenage boys | **is sitting** | **in two seats.**

Note: The verb must agree in number with the subject. If a subject is modified by a phrase beginning with a preposition, the verb usually agrees with the head word or words.

Practice

Look at the picture on page 36. Then tell what the people are doing.

1. Practically everyone on the bus ___is standing___ up.
2. A few lucky people ______________ down.
3. The two men on the left ______________ on the bus.
4. One of the men ______________ the woman who is standing near the door.
5. The older woman near the door ______________ a shopping bag.
6. The little boy ______________ a candy bar.
7. The man in the raincoat ______________ the newspaper.
8. The woman with all the packages ______________ .
9. The man next to the woman with all the packages ______________ the woman's handbag.
10. The two teenage boys ______________ to the radio.
11. One of the boys ______________ in two seats.
12. The other boy ______________ a cigarette.

Make It Work

NO SMOKING
NO LITTERING
NO RADIO PLAYING

Answer the questions.

Who's littering the bus? ______________________________

Who's smoking? ______________________________

Who's playing a radio? ______________________________

The man behind the two women was writing a check.

SUBJECT-VERB AGREEMENT

PAST CONTINUOUS

GrammarGuide
4.15

The two women [were talking] to each other.

The man behind the two women [was writing] a check.

Note: The verb must agree in number with the subject. If the subject is modified by a phrase beginning with a preposition, the verb usually agrees with the head word or words.

Practice

At 2:30 p.m. yesterday, a bank robber with a gun entered National Bank and took $250,000. No one saw the robber enter the bank. Tell what each person was doing when the robber entered the bank. Fill in the blanks with the past continuous.

1. (talk) The bank teller ___was talking___ to the woman at the teller's window.
2. (deposit) The woman at the teller's window ______________ some money in her account.
3. (stand) Two women and a man ______________ in line.
4. (talk) The two women standing in line ______________ to each other.
5. (write) The man behind the two women ______________ a check.
6. (endorse) The woman at the table near the window ______________ a check.
7. (fill) The men next to her ______________ out deposit slips.
8. (sit) The loan officer ______________ at his desk.
9. (apply) The man and woman sitting in front of the loan officer ______________ for a loan.
10. (wait) The two people sitting on the couch ______________ to see the loan officer.

Make It Work

Put a black dot (●) in the picture to show where each person was at the time of the robbery.

New Words:

endorse–sign your name on the back of a check **deposit–put in the bank**

While she was watching television, her two oldest children came home from school.

STATEMENTS WITH *WHEN* AND *WHILE*
SIMPLE PAST AND PAST CONTINUOUS

GrammarGuide
4.15
8.12

She [was reading] a book when the doorbell [rang.]
While she [was reading] a book, the doorbell [rang.]

Note: Use the past continuous for a longer, continuing action. Use the past tense for an action that interrupts a longer action.

Practice

Roberta was looking forward to a relaxing day. Her two oldest children were in school, and the baby was taking a nap.

Fill in the blanks with the correct tense of the verb in parentheses.

1. Roberta ____was resting____ (rest) when her alarm clock accidentally ____went____ (go) off.
2. She ________________ (take) a bath when the doorbell ________________ (ring).
3. While she and her next-door neighbor ________________ (have) coffee, the plumber ________________ (arrive).
4. The telephone ________________ (ring) while the plumber ________________ (talk) to her.
5. She ________________ (talk) on the telephone when the baby ________________ (start) to cry.
6. While she ________________ (feed) the baby, she ________________ (have) another telephone call.
7. She and the baby ________________ (play) in the yard when it ________________ (start) to rain.
8. She put the baby down for another nap. While she ________________ (eat) lunch, the baby ________________ (begin) to cry again.
9. She was exhausted, so she ________________ (decide) to watch television.
10. While she ________________ (watch) television, her two oldest children ________________ (come) home from school.

David will be bringing a guest.

NEGATIVE AND AFFIRMATIVE STATEMENTS
FUTURE CONTINUOUS

GrammarGuide **4.10**

Rita: I'm having a party. Can you come?
David: Of course I'll come. May I bring a guest?
Rita: Certainly.

David | will be bringing | a guest.
He | won't be coming | alone.

Practice

Rita is going to have a party. She invited fourteen people. Read each reply. Then make one negative or affirmative sentence with the future continuous.

Gloria:	I'd like to come, but I'm busy that night.	1.	Gloria won't be coming to the party.
Chris and Pascale:	We'd love to come, but we'll have to leave early.	2.	Chris and Pascale will be leaving early.
Louis:	I'll be out of town on the 14th, but thank you for asking me.	3.	______________
Pat and Cathy:	We'd love to come.	4.	______________
Mary:	Yes. It sounds like fun.	5.	______________
Laura and Paul:	Yes. We'll be there.	6.	______________
Tish:	It sounds like fun. If you've invited Paul and Laura, I'll see if I can come with them.	7.	______________
David:	Of course I'll come. May I bring a guest?	8.	______________
Gary:	Yes, but I'll probably arrive late. I have a meeting at 7:30.	9.	______________
John and his wife:	I'm sorry. We can't come. We've made other plans for the 14th.	10.	______________

Make It Work

Answer the questions.

How many people will be coming to the party? ______________

Who will be bringing a guest? ______________

You mean he's been raking the leaves for three hours?

PRESENT PERFECT CONTINUOUS

GrammarGuide
4.18

He's raking the leaves.
He started three hours ago.

You mean he 's been raking the leaves for three hours?

Note: The present perfect continuous is formed with:

have* or *has	+	***been***	+	**verb + *ing***
has		***been***		***raking***
have		***been***		***pulling***

Practice

Make questions with *you mean* and the present perfect continuous.

1. He's mowing the lawn.
   He started three hours ago.
   You mean he's been mowing the lawn for three hours?
2. She's watering the lawn.
   She started four hours ago.
3. They're pulling weeds.
   They started an hour ago.
4. She's planting flowers.
   She started two hours ago.
5. They're painting the house.
   They started six hours ago.
6. He's putting up the storm windows.
   He started two hours ago.
7. They're washing the windows.
   They started four hours ago.
8. He's fixing the driveway.
   He started three hours ago.
9. She's sweeping the patio.
   She started an hour ago.
10. He's trimming the bushes.
    He started three hours ago.

New Words:
weed–an unwanted plant which prevents flowers from growing properly
trim–make neat or even by cutting

No, thanks. I've already had dinner.

STATEMENTS WITH *ALREADY* AND *YET*
PRESENT PERFECT: IRREGULAR PAST PARTICIPLES

GrammarGuide
8.3
6.2

Irregular Past Participles

drive – driven	**choose – chosen**	**meet – met**
see – seen	**speak – spoken**	**buy – bought**
go – gone	**make – made**	**have – had**
do – done	**read – read**	

Would you like to have dinner after class? **No, thanks. I 've already had dinner.**
Yes, I would. I haven't had dinner yet.

Note: **Use *already* in affirmative statements.**
Use *yet* in negative statements.

***Have been* can be used in place of *have gone* in the perfect tenses:**
Would you like to go to the cafeteria? Sure, I haven't been there yet.

Practice

Make negative and affirmative sentences with *yet* or *already*. Answer in complete sentences.

1. Would you like to drive around the campus? — No, thanks. I've already driven around the campus.
2. Would you care to see the new language lab? — Yes, I would. I haven't seen the new language lab yet.
3. Would you like to choose an English class? — No, thanks. ______
4. Would you like to make an appointment with the foreign student adviser? — Yes, I would. ______
5. Would you like to read the student handbook? — No, thanks. ______
6. Would you like to meet the instructor? — Yes, I would. ______
7. Would you like to speak to the instructor after class? — Yes, I would. ______
8. How about going to the bookstore? — Good idea. ______
9. Would you like to buy a dictionary? — Yes, I would. ______
10. Would you like to do the homework with me? — No, thanks. ______

New Words:
campus–the grounds of a college, university, or school
handbook–a small book with important information about a particular subject

I've never heard Egyptian music.

STATEMENTS WITH *NEVER*

PRESENT PERFECT: IRREGULAR PAST PARTICIPLES

GrammarGuide
8.2
6.2

Irregular Past Participles

was/were–been	**drank–drunk**	**found–found**
flew–flown	**swam–swum**	**heard–heard**
ate–eaten		**slept–slept**
took–taken		**kept–kept**

I	**'ve never been**	**to Egypt.**
I	**'ve been**	**to Egypt.**

Note: The present perfect can be used to express an action which occurred at an unstated or unknown time in the past.

Practice

Respond to each statement. Tell if you have ever done the following things. Use *never* or *too* in your sentences.

1. My friend was in Egypt last month. I've never been to Egypt. OR I've been to Egypt too.
2. She flew on a 747. ______
3. She met an Egyptian. ______
4. She ate Egyptian food. ______
5. She drank mint tea. ______
6. She took a picture of a famous statue. ______
7. She found a piece of an old vase. ______
8. She heard Egyptian music. ______
9. She swam in the Mediterranean. ______
10. She drove through the desert. ______
11. She slept in a tent. ______
12. She kept a diary. ______

New Words:
mint–a type of plant with leaves, usually used in flavoring drinks
diary–a daily record of the events in someone's life

Have you ever ridden a camel?

QUESTIONS WITH *EVER*
PRESENT PERFECT: IRREGULAR PAST PARTICIPLES

GrammarGuide
8.2
6.2

Irregular Past Participles

rode – ridden	**spent – spent**
got – gotten	**brought – brought**
wore – worn	**stood – stood**

I've been **to Egypt.**

Have you ever been **to Egypt?**

Practice

Respond to each statement with a question. Use *you* (or *your*) in your question.

1. My friend was in Egypt last month.	Have you ever been to Egypt?
2. She spent Egyptian money.	____________
3. She went to a bazaar.	____________
4. She bought Egyptian jewelry.	____________
5. She took a boat trip up the Nile.	____________
6. She rode a camel.	____________
7. She stood in front of a temple.	____________
8. She saw the pyramids.	____________
9. She read a book on the history of Egypt.	____________
10. She got up at 4:30 to see a sunrise.	____________
11. She wore a veil.	____________
12. She brought home souvenirs of her trip.	____________

New Words:
bazaar–a market with a group of shops
temple–a building dedicated to worship

veil

pyramids

By the time Gary got there, the wedding reception had started.

AFFIRMATIVE STATEMENTS

PAST PERFECT

GrammarGuide
4.19

The wedding reception started at 5:00. Gary got there at 7:00.

By the time Gary got there, the wedding reception [had started.]

Note: **Use the past perfect tense for a past action completed before another past action.**

first action: **The wedding reception started at 5:00.**

second action: **Gary got there at 7:00.**

Irregular Past Participles

had – had	**met – met**
threw – thrown	**left – left**

Practice

Make sentences using the past perfect tense.

1. The wedding reception started. — By the time Gary got there, the wedding reception had started.
2. The guests arrived. — By the time Gary got there, ______________________
3. The guests met one another. — By the time Gary got there, ______________________
4. Everyone ate a piece of cake. — By the time Gary got there, ______________________
5. Everyone had a glass of champagne. — By the time Gary got there, ______________________
6. The band started to play. — By the time Gary got there, ______________________
7. The bride danced with the groom. — By the time Gary got there, ______________________
8. Several people left the reception. — By the time Gary got there, ______________________
9. The bride threw the bouquet. — By the time Gary got there, ______________________
10. The photographer took a lot of pictures. — By the time Gary got there, ______________________

Make It Work

Name something—a reception, a party, a meeting, a class, or a speech—that you arrived late at. Tell two things that had happened before you arrived.

I arrived late at ______________________.
By the time I ______________, ______________________.

Until last week, Mario hadn't seen snow.

NEGATIVE STATEMENTS

PAST PERFECT

GrammarGuide
4.2

Mario saw snow last week.

Until last week, Mario **hadn't seen** **snow.**

Contraction: **hadn't → had not**

Practice

Mario came to the United States for a visit last week.

Make negative sentences using the past perfect tense. Begin your sentences with *until last week* . . . .

1. Mario visited the United States. Until last week, he hadn't visited the United States.
2. He flew on a jet. ______
3. He saw snow. ______
4. He spoke English. ______
5. He met an American. ______
6. He ate a hamburger. ______
7. He drank a milk shake. ______
8. He saw pop art. ______
9. He heard country music. ______
10. He went to a barbecue. ______

Make It Work

Name a place you have visited. Then tell two things that you hadn't done before you visited that place.

Until I visited ______, ______.

______.

New Words:
pop art–modern, popular art
barbecue–a party where meat is cooked over an open fire

GrammarGuide
4.4
4.7
4.14

The couple will reside in Buckingham.

SIMPLE PRESENT, SIMPLE PAST, FUTURE WITH *WILL*

Practice

Fill in the blanks with the correct verb tense. Use the simple present, the simple past, or the future with *will*.

WEDDINGS
DeFazio-Cortina

The Union Church in Newtown ____was____ (1. be) the setting for the marriage of Jennifer Cortina and Robert DeFazio last Saturday.

The parents of the couple ________ (2. be) Mr. and Mrs. Arthur Cortina of Newtown and Mr. and Mrs. Jerry DeFazio of Buckingham.

The bride ________ (3. wear) a white wedding dress and ________ (4. carry) white daisies. The bridesmaids ________ (5. be) Mrs. John R. Wilson and Julie Cortina, sisters of the bride, and Elaine DeFazio, the groom's sister. Linda Martino ________ (6. be) the maid of honor.

Richard Cox ________ (7. serve) as best man and ushers ________ (8. be) Larry Gold and James Reed.

The bride and groom both ________ (9. graduate) from Newtown High School last June. At the present time, the bride ________ (10. work) as a dental assistant in Buckingham. The groom currently ________ (11. work) for the State of Pennsylvania. He ________ (12. be) a part-time accountant. Next fall, Mr. DeFazio ________ (13. attend) Bucks County Community College where he ________ (14. major) in accounting. After a wedding trip to Jamaica, the couple ________ (15. reside) in Buckingham.

New Word:
reside–live

When Kay and Jack were 65 years old, they decided to retire.

VERB + INFINITIVE VS. VERB + GERUND

SIMPLE PRESENT, SIMPLE PAST, FUTURE WITH *WILL*

GrammarGuide **6.4**

At first they expected [to have] nothing to do all day.

Now they don't mind [being] at home.

Note: Use the infinitive form (*to* + verb) after these verbs:

decide	**expect**	**hope**
need	**want**	

Use the gerund form (verb + *ing*) after these verbs:

appreciate	**consider**	**enjoy**	**imagine**
keep on	**mind**	**miss**	

Practice

Fill in the blanks with the correct form of the verb in parentheses.

1. (retire) When Kay and Jack were 65 years old, they decided ____to retire____.
2. (have) At first they expected ________ nothing to do all day.
3. (retire) "I can't imagine ________," said Jack. "My job is my whole life."
4. (work/do) Kay kept on ________ for a few months after Jack retired because she said she needed ________ something.
5. (be) Today they don't mind ________ at home.
6. (work) In fact, they don't miss ________ at all.
7. (swim/garden) Jack and Kay enjoy ________ and ________.
8. (do) They appreciate ________ things they never had time to do before.
9. (write/take) Jack is considering ________ a book in the future, and Kay wants ________ some cooking classes.
10. (travel) Next year, they also hope ________ to Mexico.

Make It Work

Fill in the blanks.

When I retire, I hope ________. I want ________
________. I won't miss ________
________. I'll enjoy ________.

New Word:
retire–stop working because of age

He's visited 143 countries so far. He visited 4 countries last summer.

SIMPLE PAST VS. PRESENT PERFECT

GrammarGuide
4.17

He | **visited** | **4 countries last summer.**

He | **'s visited** | **143 countries so far.**

Practice

Fill in the blanks with the past tense or the present perfect tense. Use contractions whenever possible.

People have called Jesse Hart Rosdail the world's most well-traveled man. He 's visited (1. visit) 143 of the world's 147 countries; also he ______________ (2. travel) to many territories and out-of-the-way islands. And he's still traveling. Mr. Rosdail, a sixty-year-old fifth-grade teacher from Elmhurst, Illinois, announced last week, "I ______________ (3. be) to 290 islands and countries so far."

He ______________ (4. spend) last summer visiting the Marquesas Islands in the South Pacific. He ______________ (5. fly) there three times before his plane could land.

The summer before last he ______________ (6. go) to the Santa Cruz Islands near New Guinea. He ______________ (7. hire) a private plane from the Solomon Islands to take him there. After visiting the Santa Cruz Islands, he also ______________ (8. see) the Bonin Islands near Japan. Then he ______________ (9. go) to Africa where he ______________ (10. drive) through Ethiopia and ______________ (11. visit) Djibouti on the Indian Ocean.

"It's still interesting to go to the far corners of the earth," says Mr. Rosdail. "If there's a place I ______________ (12. not/be) to, it attracts me."

Most people ______________ (13. never/travel) outside their own countries. In fact, they ______________ (14. never/hear) of most of the places Mr. Rosdail ______________ (15. be) to.

New Word:
territory–an area of land ruled by one government

Is the stereo absolutely free? No, it isn't.

SAM'S STEREO CENTER

336 George Avenue
Paterson, New Jersey

HERE IS YOUR CHANCE TO RECEIVE A FREE
MAJESTIC STEREO!

You will receive a beautiful new stereo absolutely FREE, based on the number of records you purchase from our huge selection of famous artists. You only have to purchase one record album a week for six months to receive a stereo. You don't have to pay for the records you purchase right now. You can pay later.

This offer is good for only seven days. Selection of stereos is limited, so visit our store soon.

Wishing you a lifetime of listening pleasure.

Very truly yours,

E. F. Stanley

Advertising Manager

Sam's Stereo Center
Store hours

Mon.–Fri. 10:00 a.m.–9:00 p.m.
Sat. 9:00 a.m.–6:00 p.m.

Record albums are $20.00.

No deliveries.

Is the stereo absolutely free? No, it isn't.

NEGATIVE AND AFFIRMATIVE SHORT ANSWERS
SIMPLE PRESENT, FUTURE WITH *WILL*

GrammarGuide
4.2

Is the stereo absolutely free? No, it isn't.

Do you have to purchase something in order to get a free stereo? Yes, you do.

Note: *You* is used in a general sense to mean *anyone*, especially in speech. When a question contains *you* used in a general sense, use *you* in your answer.

Practice

Look at the letter on page 50. Then give a negative or affirmative short answer for each question.

1. Is the stereo absolutely free? No, it isn't.
2. Do you have to purchase something in order to receive a free stereo? Yes, you do.
3. Is $20.00 a reasonable price for a record album? ____________
4. Does a record album usually cost $20.00? ____________
5. If you purchase one album a week for six months, will you have to buy twenty-six record albums? ____________
6. Will it cost a lot of money to get the stereo? ____________
7. Do you have to pay for the records now? ____________
8. Can you pay later? ____________
9. Is it possible to buy a stereo for $500? ____________
10. Is Majestic a well-known name in stereos? ____________
11. Are there many stereo styles to choose from? ____________
12. Will they deliver the new stereo? ____________
13. Is this offer good next month? ____________
14. Is this offer a good deal for someone who wants to buy some records? ____________
15. Is this offer a good deal for someone who needs a stereo? ____________

New Words:
selection–choice
limited–lasting only for a specified amount of time

You remember Dee Williams, don't you?

TAG QUESTIONS

SIMPLE PRESENT, SIMPLE PAST, FUTURE, PRESENT CONTINUOUS, PRESENT PERFECT CONTINUOUS, PAST PERFECT

GrammarGuide **4.2**

She worked in customer service, didn't she?

She has blond hair, doesn't she?

You remember her now, don't you?

Note: **The first part of a tag question is a statement, and the second part is a question. When the statement is positive, the attached question is negative.**

Practice

Fill in the dialogue with tag questions.

Barbara: You remember Dee Williams, don't you? (1.)

Mary: I think so. She used to work here, ____________ (2.)

Barbara: Yes, she did.

Mary: She worked in customer service, ____________ (3.)

Barbara: I'm not sure. She was in the promotion department, ____________ (4.)

Mary: She's tall and thin, ____________ (5.)

Barbara: No. You're thinking of someone else. Dee's short.

Mary: Oh, I remember her now. She worked here about a year ago,

____________ (6.)

Barbara: Yes.

Mary: When she quit, she had been here a long time, ____________ (7.)

Barbara: Yes. Maybe she had worked here for five years. I'm not sure.

Mary: She's working for an advertising agency now, ____________ (8.)

Barbara: Yes, I believe so.

Mary: She's been working there since she left A.B.C., ____________ (9.)

Barbara: Yes. Anyway, she'll be coming into the office tomorrow.

Mary: Really? I'll be interested in seeing her, ____________ (10.)

If you buy a new car now, you'll get a rebate.

AFFIRMATIVE STATEMENTS
FUTURE REAL CONDITIONAL

GrammarGuide
4.23
8.14

If you [present] this card at our shop, you ['ll get] a free gift.

Note: The future real conditional is used to express a situation that is expected as a result of some condition or requirement.

Use the present tense for the condition. Use the future tense for the result.

***You* is used in general statements to mean *anyone*.**

Punctuation: *If* ______ [,] ______.

Practice

Make sentences using the future real conditional.

1. Purchase any Jabot product for $10.00 or more. Get a free bottle of cologne.	If you purchase any Jabot product for $10.00 or more, you'll get a free bottle of cologne.
2. Visit our shop. Receive a free gift.	
3. Buy a new car now. Get a $250 rebate.	
4. Call this number now. Get a set of steak knives.	
5. Subscribe to *Now* magazine. Save 50% on the regular price.	
6. Fill in your name and birthdate. Receive a free necklace.	
7. Visit our pharmacy. Get $1.00 off on any prescription.	
8. Open a new account at Century Savings. Receive a free set of dishes.	
9. Buy three bars of soap. Get one absolutely free.	
10. Present this coupon at your grocery store. Save 50¢ on your next purchase of Homestyle Potato Chips.	

New Words:
rebate–a return of part of a payment
subscribe–pay regularly in order to receive a magazine or newspaper
present–show

If I were a bird, I'd like to be a swan.

AFFIRMATIVE STATEMENTS

PRESENT UNREAL CONDITIONAL

GrammarGuide
4.23
8.14

If I [were] a bird, I ['d like] to be a swan.

Note: The present unreal conditional is used to express possibilities in the present.

Contraction: I'd → I would

Punctuation: *If* ______ [,] ______.

Practice

For each of the following general categories, name something specific you'd like to be. Begin your sentences with *if.*

1. a bird — If I were a bird, I'd like to be a swan.
2. a fish ________________
3. an animal ________________
4. a flower ________________
5. a car ________________
6. a musical instrument ________________
7. a city ________________
8. an island ________________
9. a river ________________
10. a country ________________

Make It Work

Name one thing you'd like to be. Then tell why you'd like to be that thing.

I'd like to be a swan because swans are graceful.

____

____

If I won a million dollars, I'd take a trip around the world.

CONTRAST: PRESENT UNREAL AND FUTURE REAL CONDITIONALS

GrammarGuide **4.23**

Real Condition:	**If I**	**take**	**a vacation for two weeks, I**	**'ll go**	**to Maine.**
Unreal Condition:	**If I**	**took**	**a vacation for two months, I**	**'d go**	**to Egypt.**

Practice

Below is a list of some of the things people want out of life. Put a check next to all the activities that will probably happen to you in the near future. Then make sentences with *if* for all of the phrases.

✓ 1. take a vacation for two weeks — If I take a vacation for two weeks, I'll go to the beach.

___ 2. take a vacation for two months — If I took a vacation for two months, I'd go to Morocco.

___ 3. buy a new car ______________________

___ 4. own a sailboat ______________________

___ 5. move to the country ______________________

___ 6. be famous ______________________

___ 7. buy a new television ______________________

___ 8. have a swimming pool ______________________

___ 9. win a million dollars ______________________

___ 10. go back to school ______________________

___ 11. save some money ______________________

___ 12. lose weight ______________________

If I had been King Edward of England, I wouldn't have given up my throne for a woman.

NEGATIVE AND AFFIRMATIVE STATEMENTS
PAST UNREAL CONDITIONAL

GrammarGuide
4.23
8.14

If I [had been] Grace Kelly, I [would / wouldn't have given up] my movie career to marry a prince.

Note: Use *if* + the past perfect tense + *would have* + the past participle for unreal possibilities in the past.

Contraction: wouldn't → would not

Punctuation: *If* ______ [,] ______.

Practice

If you had been each of the following people, would you or wouldn't you have done what they did? Use negative or affirmative sentences.

1. Grace Kelly gave up her movie career to marry a prince. — If I had been Grace Kelly, I wouldn't have given up my movie career to marry a prince.
2. Thomas Becket died for his church. ______________________
3. Susan B. Anthony fought for women's rights. ______________________
4. King Henry VIII had seven wives. ______________________
5. Jean-Paul Sartre refused the Nobel Prize. ______________________
6. King Edward of England gave up his throne for a woman. ______________________
7. Joan of Arc died for her country. ______________________
8. Martin Luther King fought for civil rights. ______________________

New Words:
Nobel Prize–an important prize given in Sweden each year for work in science and literature
throne–the chair of a king or queen
civil rights–the rights which belong to a person because he or she is a citizen

If she hadn't woken up late, she wouldn't have been in a hurry.

NEGATIVE STATEMENTS
PAST UNREAL CONDITIONAL

GrammarGuide
8.14

She woke up late. She was in a hurry.

If she [hadn't woken up] late, she [wouldn't have been] in a hurry.

Note: Use the past unreal conditional for an unreal possibility in the past.
condition: if she hadn't woken up late
result: she wouldn't have been in a hurry

Contractions: hadn't → had not
wouldn't → would not

Punctuation: *If* ______ [,] ______.

Practice

Make negative sentences in the past unreal conditional.

1. She woke up late. She was in a hurry. — If she hadn't woken up late, she wouldn't have been in a hurry.
2. She was in a hurry. She had to run to the train station. ______________________
3. She had to run to the train station. She slipped on the ice. ______________________
4. She slipped on the ice. Her briefcase flew open. ______________________
5. Her briefcase flew open. Her papers were scattered everywhere. ______________________
6. Her papers were scattered everywhere. She had to pick them up. ______________________
7. She had to pick them up. She arrived at the train station late. ______________________
8. She arrived at the train station late. She missed her train. ______________________
9. She missed her train. She arrived at the office late. ______________________
10. She arrived at the office late. Her boss was angry. ______________________

New Words:
fly open–open suddenly with force
scatter–separate in all directions

I should do my homework, but I'd rather read a book.

SHOULD VS. *WOULD RATHER*

GrammarGuide
5.10
5.14

I [should do] my homework, but I ['d rather read] a book.

Note: Use *would rather* to express a preference where a choice is given. Use *should* to show that an action is advisable.

Contraction: I'd → I would

Practice

Look at each choice of activities. First tell what you *should* do. Then tell what you*'d rather* do. Join your sentences with a comma (,) and *but*.

1. read a book
   do my homework
   I should do my homework, but I'd rather read a book.
2. do the laundry
   go to the movies
   ____
3. watch the baseball game
   clean the house
   ____
4. mow the lawn
   take a nap
   ____
5. fix dinner
   go out
   ____
6. stay in bed
   get up early
   ____
7. drink a glass of milk
   have some soda
   ____
8. do the dishes
   watch television
   ____
9. stay home
   go to work
   ____
10. go to the party
    do my work
    ____

Make It Work

Make two sentences about this weekend. First tell what you *should* do. Then tell what you*'d rather* do instead.

____
____
____

You must not get up and walk around.

HAVE TO, DON'T HAVE TO, AND *MUST NOT*

GrammarGuide
5.16

You | **have to** | **fasten your seat belt.**

You | **must not** | **get up and walk around.**

You | **don't have to** | **fasten your seat belt.**

Note: ***have to* and *must* = obligation**
***must not* = prohibition**
***don't have to* = lack of necessity**

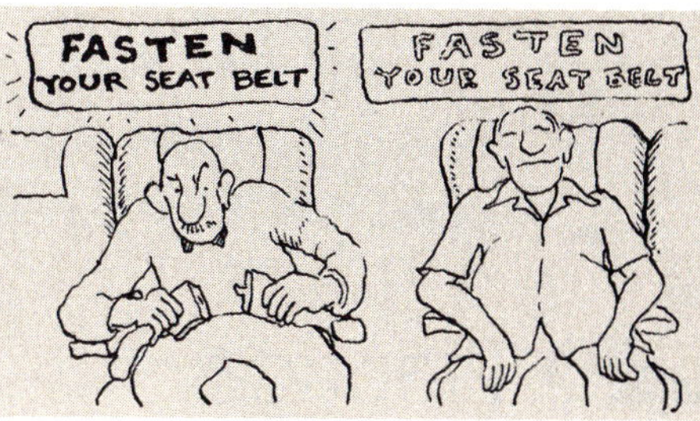

Practice

Fill in the blanks with *have to, don't have to,* or *must not.* Read the entire sentence first.

1. You ___have to___ be at the airport early to reserve a seat. Otherwise, you might not get a seat on the plane.
2. You ________________ check your suitcase. You can't carry it on the plane.
3. You ________________ check your briefcase or purse. You can carry hand luggage on the plane if you like.
4. You ________________ put your hand luggage under your seat.
5. You ________________ leave anything in the aisles.
6. You ________________ fasten your seat belt when the plane takes off and lands.
7. You ________________ get up and walk around when the "fasten your seat belt" sign is on.
8. You ________________ keep your seat belt fastened the entire time. You can get up and walk around after the "fasten your seat belt" sign goes off.
9. You ________________ smoke when the plane takes off and lands.
10. If you want to smoke, you ________________ sit in the smoking section.

Make It Work

Name two important rules for a passenger who flies on an airplane.

You ____

You ____

New Words:
reserve–keep for future use
entire–whole

aisle 

She could take a nap.

OPPORTUNITY WITH *COULD*

GrammarGuide **5.7**

Phil is hungry. There's chicken and hamburger in the refrigerator.

He [could have] chicken.

Note: Use *could* to show that an opportunity exists in the present or future.

Practice

Make sentences with *could*.

Mako is sleepy.
1. She could take a nap.
2. She could drink some coffee.

Rafael and Conchita are bored.
3. __________
4. __________

Dennis is broke.
5. __________
6. __________

Nick is lonely.
7. __________
8. __________

Louise and Raymond are lost.
9. __________
10. __________

Martine is in trouble.
11. __________
12. __________

Make It Work

Simon is broke. He has no money to go out Saturday night. What are some things he could do that don't cost any money?

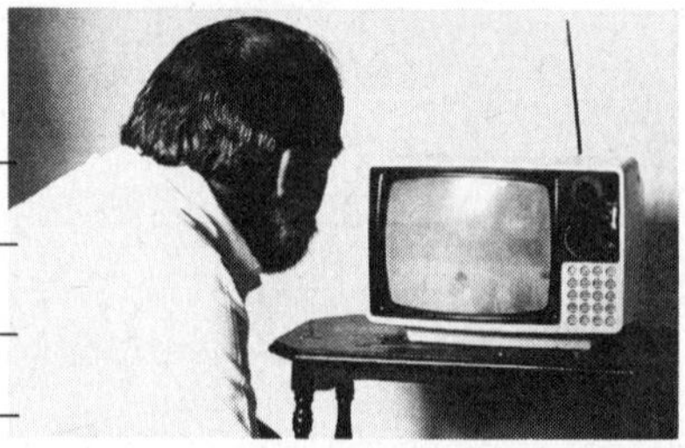

He could watch television.

____

____

____

It could be a rainbow. It might be a rainbow.

POSSIBILITY WITH *COULD* AND *MIGHT*

GrammarGuide
5.7
5.12

What is this?

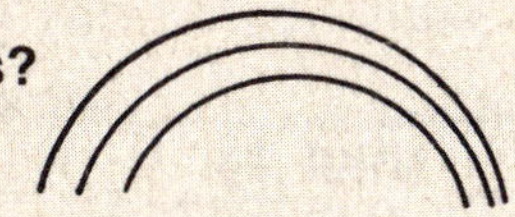

It | **could be** | **a rainbow.**
It | **might be** | **a rainbow.**

Note: Use *could* or *might* for present possibility.

Practice

What could each of the following items be? Suggest two different possibilities for each item. Make one sentence with *could* and another with *might*.

1. It could be a package with a bow.
2. It might be a shirt with a bow tie.

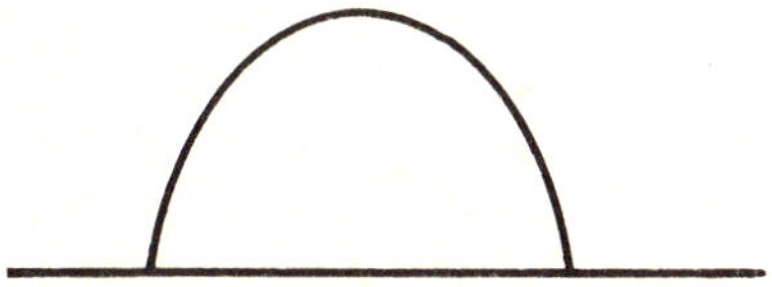

3. ______________________________
4. ______________________________

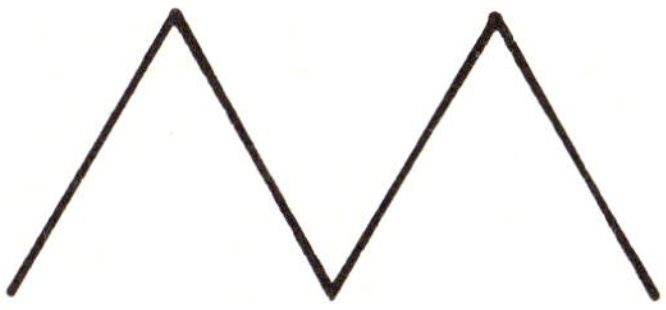

5. ______________________________
6. ______________________________

7. ______________________________
8. ______________________________

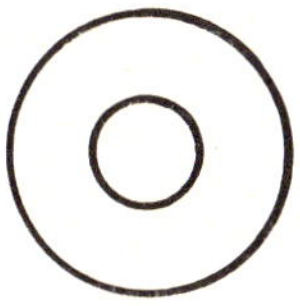

9. ______________________________
10. ______________________________

They used to work eight hours a day.

USED TO

GrammarGuide
5.9

Kay and Jack [used to work] eight hours a day.
Now they don't work. They're retired.

Note: ***Used to*** **expresses a recurring action in the past:**
used to **+ the simple form of the verb**
used to live

Practice

Fill in the blanks with *used to* and the appropriate verb. Be sure to read both sentences first.

Kay and Jack are retired.

1. They ___used to live___ in a house.
   Now they live in an apartment.
2. They both ______________ eight hours a day.
   Now they don't work anymore.
3. They ______________ in a big city.
   Now they live in a small town.
4. They never ______________ time gardening.
   Now they spend a lot of time gardening.
5. They never ______________ courses.
   Now they both take courses at the community college.
6. They never ______________ swimming.
   Now they go swimming every day.
7. Kay never ______________ her own pottery.
   Now she makes her own pottery.
8. Jack never ______________ interested in writing.
   Now Jack is interested in writing.
9. They never ______________ vacations.
   Now they take vacations three or four times a year.
10. They never ______________ time to enjoy themselves.
    Now they have time to enjoy themselves.

Make It Work

Name two things that you never used to do.

____

____

New Word:
pottery–pots made of clay

She isn't used to living in the city.

BE USED TO

GrammarGuide **7.9**

Betsy lived in the suburbs.

She | **isn't used to living** | **in the city.**

Note: ***be used to* = be accustomed to:**
to be* + *used to* + verb + *ing
is used to living

Practice

Betsy used to live with her parents in the suburbs. Now she lives in the city and has a job.

Fill in the blanks with *be used to* and the appropriate verb. Be sure to read both sentences first.

1. She lived in the suburbs.
   She <u>isn't used to living</u> in the city.
2. She didn't work.
   She ______________________ from 9:00 to 5:00.
3. She commuted to school by car.
   She ______________________ to work by subway.
4. She lived with her parents.
   She ______________________ alone.
5. She lived in a house.
   She ______________________ in an apartment.
6. Her mother cooked all her meals.
   She ______________________ all her own meals.
7. Her mother cleaned the house.
   She ______________________ her apartment.
8. Her mother did the laundry.
   She ______________________ the laundry.
9. Her parents supported her.
   She ______________________ herself.
10. She didn't pay her own bills.
    She ______________________ her own bills.

New Word:
support–provide money for a person to live

She should have taken her money with her.

SHOULD HAVE

GrammarGuide
5.14

She didn't turn the heat down before she left the house.

She [should have turned] the heat down before she left the house.

Note: Use *should* + *have* + the past participle to express an action that was advisable but did not occur.

Irregular Past Participles:
feed–fed take–taken

Practice

Angela left the house in a hurry this morning.

Make sentences with *should have.*

1. She didn't turn the heat down. She should have turned the heat down.
2. She didn't turn off the lights. ____________________
3. She didn't feed the dog. ____________________
4. She didn't close the windows. ____________________
5. She didn't take out the trash. ____________________
6. She didn't make sure the oven was off. ____________________
7. She didn't turn the radio off. ____________________
8. She didn't lock all the doors. ____________________
9. She didn't take her keys with her. ____________________
10. She didn't take her money with her. ____________________

Make It Work

Name two things you should have done this morning before you left the house.

____

____

She could have had an accident.

PAST POSSIBILITY WITH *COULD HAVE*

GrammarGuide **5.7**

I stepped on a piece of glass.

You [could have cut] your foot.

Note: Use *could have* + the past participle for past possibility. (*Might have* can also be used for past possibility.)

Irregular Past Participles:
fall–fallen catch–caught shoot–shot

Practice

Make sentences with *could have* and the words in parentheses.

1. I stepped on a piece of broken glass. (cut your foot) You could have cut your foot.
2. She climbed the broken ladder. (fall off the ladder) ____________________
3. They went outside in the snow without their jackets. (catch a cold) ____________________
4. I moved the furniture by myself. (hurt your back) ____________________
5. She didn't stop at the traffic light. (have an accident) ____________________
6. He crossed the street against the light. (be hit by a car) ____________________
7. The children were playing with a gun. (shoot someone) ____________________
8. They skied down the icy hill. (get hurt) ____________________
9. She turned on the radio with her wet hands. (get a shock) ____________________
10. The little boy went swimming by himself. (drown) ____________________

New Words:
shock–the effect of electricity passing through your body
drown–die by being underwater for a long time

Could you have left it in your pocket?

CONTRAST: MODAL AND VERB FORM REVIEW
SIMPLE FORM VS. PAST PARTICIPLE FORM

GrammarGuide
5.17

Simple Form	Past Participle Form
should + take	should have + taken
have to + take	must have + taken
did (you) + take	have + taken
didn't + take	have (you) + taken
don't + take	haven't + taken

Irregular Past Participle: lay–laid

Practice

Fill in the blanks with the correct form of the verb in parentheses.

Amanda: I lost my ring.

Dotty: Where did you ____put____ (1. put) it?

Amanda: I don't know. I was washing the dishes in the kitchen.

Dotty: Well, then it must ____________ (2. be) in the kitchen. Why don't you ____________ (3. look) in the kitchen?

Amanda: I did, but it wasn't there. I must have ____________ (4. lay) it down somewhere else.

Dotty: Is it in the bathroom? It could ____________ (5. be) there.

Amanda: No. I checked the bathroom. I took it off, but I can't ____________ (6. remember) where I put it.

Dotty: How about your pocket? Could you have ____________ (7. leave) it in your pocket?

Amanda: No. I looked.

Dotty: You should ____________ (8. look) every place that you've been today.

Amanda: I have ____________ (9. look) everywhere. It's lost. I shouldn't have ____________ (10. take) it off.

Dotty: I'd like to ____________ (11. help) you find it, but you mustn't ____________ (12. get) upset. You have to ____________ (13. stay) calm. Let's ____________ (14. make) a list of every place you've been today. I'm sure we'll ____________ (15. find) it.

This fabulous hotel is located right on the beach.

SIMPLE PRESENT

VERB *TO BE* + PAST PARTICIPLE

GrammarGuide **4.26**

This fabulous hotel [is located] right on the beach.

All guests [are treated] to first-class accommodations.

Note: Use *am, is,* or *are* + the past participle to form present passive constructions.

Irregular Past Participle: know–known

Practice

Fill in the blanks with *is* or *are* and a past participle.

Come to Hawaii. Visit the Kauai Surf Hotel for as little as $50.00 a day per person!

1. (locate) This fabulous hotel __is located__ right on the beach.
2. (know) It ________ for its beautiful rooms overlooking the ocean.
3. (treat) All guests ________ to first-class accommodations.
4. (decorate) Each room ______ tastefully ________ and has a balcony.
5. (locate) For your convenience, shops and restaurants ________ within the hotel.
6. (provide) Transportation to and from the hotel ________ free of charge.
7. (include) All hotel meals ________ in the price of your room.
8. (limit) You must act now. This offer ________ .
9. (require) Reservations ________ ten days in advance.
10. (accept) All major credit cards ________ .

Treat yourself. Telephone your travel agent for further details.

New Words:
accommodations–a place to sleep, food, and services
provide–supply
limit–last only for a specified amount of time

The house was built in 1841.

SIMPLE PAST: NEGATIVE AND AFFIRMATIVE STATEMENTS
VERB *TO BE* + PAST PARTICIPLE

GrammarGuide
4.27
6.2

The house | **was built** | **in 1841.**

It | **wasn't built** | **for a rich family.**

Note: To form the past passive voice, use *was* or *were* + the past participle.

Irregular Past Participles:
build–built   make–made   buy–bought

Practice

Fill in the blanks with the past of the verb *to be* + the past participle.

The house in the picture below ___was built___ (1. build) in 1841. It looks very elegant, but it ________ (2. not/build) for a rich family. It ________ (3. build) for a middle-class family. It ________ (4. not/design) by an architect. The style ________ (5. copy) from several other houses in the area.

Today this beautiful house is an expensive apartment building, but it ________ (6. not/use) as an apartment building a hundred years ago. It ________ (7. design) for one family. Originally, it ________ (8. not/paint) as it is today. The door had a beautiful design, but the design ________ (9. remove) in 1970. The area above the door ________ (10. not/make) of brick. It ________ (11. make) of marble. In 1970, when the house ________ (12. buy) by its present owner, all the windows ________ (13. replace). In fact, in 1970, the entire house ________ (14. remodel). At that time, many old features of the house ________ (15. replace) with newer, more modern features. Still, the old house is elegant and charming.

New Words:
remove–take away
marble–a hard, polished stone
remodel–rebuild in a new form
replace–change something for something else

Her supervisor was notified about the accident.

ACTIVE VOICE VS. PASSIVE VOICE

SIMPLE PAST

GrammarGuide
4.25

Her supervisor **was notified** **about the accident.**

The doctor **notified** **her supervisor about the accident.**

Note: Use the passive voice when you don't know who performed the action or when the actor is not as important as the action. *By* is sometimes used with the passive voice.

Use the active voice when the person who performed the action is important.

Practice

Fill in the blanks with the past tense or the past passive voice.

As Mrs. McCormack was walking to work one morning, she ___was hit___ (1. hit) by a car. A person who happened to be walking by ___saw___ (2. see) the accident and ________ (3. call) an ambulance. Within minutes, the ambulance ________ (4. arrive), and Mrs. McCormack ________ (5. rush) to the hospital.

At the hospital, a doctor ________ (6. examine) her, and an X-ray ________ (7. take). Mrs. McCormack ________ (8. not/injure) badly. Her arm ________ (9. bruise), but it ________ (10. not/break). The doctor ________ (11. tell) her to go home and rest. Her supervisor at work ________ (12. notify) about the accident.

Make It Work

Tell about an accident you had.

____

____

____

New Word:
bruised–injured by a blow but not broken

Dinner will be served at 8:00.

FUTURE

PASSIVE VOICE

GrammarGuide **4.25**

We will provide transportation to the meeting.

Transportation to the meeting | **will be provided.** |

Note: The future passive voice is formed with *will* + *be* + past participle.

Irregular past participles: eat–eaten give–given hold–held

Practice

Change the sentences to the passive voice.

1. The company will hold a sales meeting on September 10th. — A sales meeting will be held on September 10th.
2. We will hold the meeting at the Manor Hotel. ______
3. We will expect all salespeople to attend. ______
4. We will provide transportation. ______
5. We will discuss sales from 9:00 to 11:00. ______
6. Someone will give a sales report from 11:00 to 12:00. ______
7. We will eat lunch from 12:00 to 1:00. ______
8. We will divide the people into two groups from 2:00 to 4:00. ______
9. We will give a cocktail party at 5:00. ______
10. The hotel will serve dinner at 8:00. ______

Make It Work

The president of your company says to you, "We will hold an important meeting tomorrow at 3:00 in the conference room. I will expect all employees to attend. Send a memo." Write a memo.

TO: All Employees DATE: ______
FROM: The President

An important meeting ______. ______

______.

New Word: provide–supply

I have my teeth checked once a year.

CAUSATIVES

REGULAR AND IRREGULAR PAST PARTICIPLES AFTER *HAVE*

GrammarGuide
6.7

I [have] my hair [cut] once a month.
twice a month.
once every six months.

Note: To form the causative, use *have* or *has* + noun or pronoun + past participle.

Practice

Answer the questions in complete sentences. Tell about yourself.

1. How often do you have your hair cut? I have my hair cut three times a year.
2. How often do you have a prescription filled? ______________________
3. How often do you have your clothes dry-cleaned? ______________________
4. How often do you have your watch repaired? ______________________
5. How often do you have your teeth checked? ______________________
6. How often do you have your eyes examined? ______________________
7. How often do you have your passport renewed? ______________________
8. How often do you have your car serviced? ______________________
9. How often do you have your shoes fixed? ______________________
10. How often do you have a new key made? ______________________

Make It Work

Answer the questions.

Do you have your apartment (or house) cleaned, or do you clean it yourself? ______________________

Do you have your newspaper delivered, or do you buy it at a newsstand? ______________________

Air pollution comes from automobiles, buses, and trucks.

COMPOUND SUBJECTS AND OBJECTS
SIMPLE PRESENT, PRESENT CONTINUOUS

GrammarGuide
10.2

Air pollution comes from automobiles [and] buses.

Air pollution comes from automobiles [,] buses [,] [and] trucks.

Note: Both subjects and objects can be joined in the following way:
two items: ______ *and* ______
three items or more: ______ , ______ , *and* ______

The last comma is optional.

Practice

Combine the sentences.

1. Air pollution is a serious problem in almost every country.
   Water pollution is a serious problem in almost every country.
   Noise pollution is a serious problem in almost every country.

   Air pollution, water pollution, and noise pollution are serious problems in almost every country.

2. Air pollution comes from incinerators.
   Air pollution comes from smokestacks.

   ____

3. It also comes from automobiles.
   It also comes from buses.
   It also comes from trucks.

   ____

Air pollution comes from automobiles, buses, and trucks.

4. Water pollution comes from chemical waste.
   Water pollution comes from trash.
5. People throw trash into our rivers.
   People throw trash into our lakes.
   People throw trash into our oceans.
6. Factories dump chemical waste into our water.
   Factories dump oil into our water.
   Factories dump detergents into our water.
7. Noise pollution comes from cars.
   Noise pollution comes from car horns.
   Noise pollution comes from subways.
8. Also, construction work can cause noise pollution.
   Also, loud radios can cause noise pollution.
9. Our world is becoming unhealthy for people.
   Our world is becoming unhealthy for animals.
10. However, people can do something about it.
    However, companies can do something about it.
    However, the government can do something about it.

Make It Work

Answer the questions.

Where does air pollution come from in your city?

What are the reasons for water pollution in your city?

New Words:

incinerator 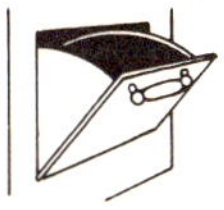 **smokestack**  **chemical waste** 

dump—drop or unload something carelessly

He didn't make a good impression in the interview, so Mr. Simon isn't going to hire him.

COMPOUND SENTENCES WITH *AND, SO,* AND *BUT*

SIMPLE PRESENT, SIMPLE PAST, FUTURE WITH *GOING TO*

GrammarGuide
10.3

Buzz can't type [,] [and] he can't take shorthand.

Yukiko can type [,] [but] she can't take shorthand.

Carlos is the most qualified [,] [so] Mr. Simon is going to offer the job to Carlos.

Note: *But* shows a contrast to the first sentence.
***So* shows a result of the first sentence.**
Punctuation: ____ [,] *and* ____. ____ [,] *but* ____.

Practice

Buzz, Yukiko, María, and Carlos all applied for a secretarial position. Mr. Simon interviewed all of them, and this is what he thinks.

Combine the sentences with *and*, *so*, or *but*.

1. Buzz can't type very well. He can't take shorthand.	Buzz can't type very well, and he can't take shorthand.
2. He didn't make a good impression in the interview. Mr. Simon isn't going to hire him.	He didn't make a good impression in the interview, so Mr. Simon isn't going to hire him.
3. Yukiko can type. She can't take shorthand.	
4. She was pleasant and polite in the interview. Mr. Simon isn't going to hire her.	
5. She can't take shorthand. She doesn't have any experience.	
6. María can type. She can take shorthand.	
7. She didn't make a good impression in the interview. Mr. Simon isn't going to hire her.	
8. Carlos can take shorthand. He can type.	
9. He was pleasant and polite in the interview. He has a lot of experience.	
10. Carlos is the best person for the job. Mr. Simon is going to offer the job to Carlos.	

Variety shows are more entertaining.

ADJECTIVE COMPARATIVES

SIMPLE PRESENT

GrammarGuide
7.5

Documentaries and the news are both educational.

I think that the news is [more educational.]

funny – funn [ier]

educational – [more educational]

Note: **Add *-er* to most two-syllable adjectives ending in *y*. Change the *y* to *i* before adding *-er*.**

Put *more* before adjectives with three or more syllables.
Notice that *news* is singular.

Practice

Make comparative sentences. Begin your sentences with *I think that*.

1. Variety shows and game shows are both entertaining. — I think that variety shows are more entertaining.
2. Situation comedies and cartoons are both funny. ____________
3. Talk shows and documentaries are both educational. ____________
4. Situation comedies and variety shows are both amusing. ____________
5. Commercials and game shows are both silly. ____________
6. Documentaries and the news are both informative. ____________
7. Old movies and soap operas are both interesting. ____________
8. Mystery stories and horror movies are both terrifying. ____________
9. Sports programs and crime dramas are both exciting. ____________
10. Situation comedies and crime dramas are both popular. ____________

Make It Work

8 PM [2] **Dan Slick, Private Investigator—Crime Drama**
[7] **Movie—Drama** "Casablanca" (1942)

There are two shows on at 8:00. Which show would you watch?
I'd watch ____________ because ____________ .

It has the most exciting roller coaster ride in the world.

ADJECTIVE SUPERLATIVES

SIMPLE PRESENT, FUTURE WITH *WILL*

GrammarGuide **7.5**

It has the most exciting roller coaster ride in the world.

	-est	-iest	most
	great – great est	**mighty – might iest**	**exotic – most exotic**
	big – big gest	**pretty – prett iest**	
Note:	**Add *-est* to most one-syllable adjectives.** **If the adjective ends in one vowel + one consonant, double the consonant.**	**Add *-est* to most two-syllable adjectives ending in *y*. Change the *y* to *i* and add *-est*.**	**Put *the most* before adjectives with three or more syllables.**

Irregular Superlative Form: good–the best

Practice

Fill in the blanks with the correct superlative form.

You will have ______the greatest______ (1. great) experience of your life at Wonder World Amusement Park. It is ____________________ (2. large) amusement park in the world. It has sixty of ____________________ (3. mighty) and ____________________ (4. exotic) animals in the world.

Wonder World has ____________________ (5. exciting) roller coaster ride in the world. It even takes you through water.

It has one of ____________________ (6. big) hot-air balloons in in the United States. It's over ten stories high. It has ____________________ (7. brave) acrobats you will ever see.

It has the most exciting roller coaster ride in the world.

It has ____________ (8. tall) and ____________ (9. spectacular) ferris wheel in the world. It's over twenty stories high, and it gives you a view of one of ____________ (10. pretty) parks in the United States.

It has one of ____________ (11. fantastic) restaurants. It has everything from ____________ (12. delicious) steaks in the world to ____________ (13. good) hot dogs in America. ____________ (14. wonderful) day of your life is only minutes away. The price for an entire day at Wonder World Amusement Park is only $16.95. (It's also ____________ (15. expensive) amusement park in the world!)

Make It Work

Make up an advertisement for each of the following products. Use superlative forms (*-est* or *the most*).

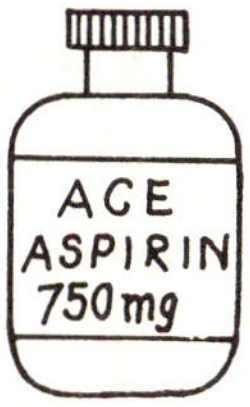

Ready Cola is the most refreshing soft drink of all.

____

____

____

____

I thought it was boring. I was bored.

ADJECTIVES ENDING IN *-ED* AND *-ING*

SIMPLE PAST

GrammarGuide **7.3**

I thought it was **boring.**
It was **disappointing.**

I was **bored.**
I was **disappointed.**

Practice

Fill in the dialogue with the correct form of the adjective.

Dave: Wasn't Wonder World Amusement Park ____boring____ ?
(1. bored/boring)

Phil: Were you ______________ ? I thought it was great. The roller coaster
(2. bored/boring)
ride was really ______________ .
(3. excited/exciting)

Dave: I didn't think so. I was ______________ .
(4. disappointed/disappointing)

Phil: Didn't you like the balloon ride?

Dave: No. I thought it was ______________ .
(5. bored/boring)

Phil: You liked the ferris wheel ride, didn't you?

Dave: No. Not after we had to wait in line for an hour. By the time I got on the ferris wheel, I was ______________ .
(6. exhausted/exhausting)

Phil: What about the acrobats? Wasn't that an ______________ act?
(7. amazed/amazing)

Dave: You're joking. I wasn't ______________ . I thought it was
(8. amazed/amazing)
______________ . You know, the man almost got killed.
(9. terrified/terrifying)

Phil: Well, you must admit it was ______________ .
(10. entertained/entertaining)

Dave: The most entertaining part of the amusement park was the restaurant!

There was no electricity in Queens.

ANY, NO, AND THE PRONOUN *NONE*
SIMPLE PRESENT, SIMPLE PAST

GrammarGuide
3.6
7.4

There wasn't [any] electricity in Queens.
There was [no] electricity in Queens.
There was [none.]

Note: Use *no* and *any* before nouns. Use *none* in place of a noun.
Do not use *no* or *none* after a negative word.

Practice

Fill in the dialogue with *any, no,* or *none.*

Sally: I'm sorry I couldn't come to work yesterday. There was ___no___ (1.) subway service in Queens.

Boss: What? Why wasn't there ________ (2.) subway service?

Sally: Didn't you hear? There wasn't ________ (3.) electricity in Queens.

Boss: You mean there was ________ (4.) electricity in the subway?

Sally: That's right. There was ________ (5.) . There wasn't ________ (6.) power at my house, either.

Boss: That's unbelievable. You mean there wasn't ________ (7.) electricity in the stores?

Sally: There was ________ (8.) .

Boss: Not ________ (9.) electricity?

Sally: ________ (10.) at all. There was a total power failure in Queens.

Boss: Wasn't there ________ (11.) way for you to get to work?

Sally: I don't have a car. I had ________ (12.) way to get here.

I don't like people who complain all the time.

ESSENTIAL ADJECTIVE CLAUSES WITH *WHO*

SIMPLE PRESENT

GrammarGuide
7.10

adjective clause

I don't like people | **who talk a lot.** |

Note: **An adjective clause modifies a noun or pronoun in the main clause of a sentence.**
Who, which, **or *that* introduces an adjective clause. Use *who* or *that* to refer to people.**

Practice

Complete the sentences with adjective clauses introduced by *who.*

1. I like people who are good listeners.
2. I dislike people ______________________________
3. I notice people ______________________________
4. I admire people ______________________________
5. I don't trust people ______________________________
6. I don't understand people ______________________________
7. I feel uncomfortable with people ______________________________
8. I don't approve of people ______________________________
9. I get angry at people ______________________________
10. I enjoy being around people ______________________________
11. I am impressed by people ______________________________
12. I am bored by people ______________________________

Make It Work

Fill in the blanks with a main clause and an adjective clause.

I ____________________ men ______________________________ .

I ____________________ women ______________________________ .

I ____________________ children ______________________________ .

New Words:
admire–have respect for
trust–believe in the honesty of
approve of–consider good
impress–fill with admiration

I like houses which are easy to clean.

VERB AGREEMENT IN ESSENTIAL ADJECTIVE CLAUSES WITH *WHICH* OR *THAT*

SIMPLE PRESENT

GrammarGuide **3.11** **7.10**

I like houses	**which are easy to clean.**
I like houses	**that are easy to clean.**
I like furniture	**that is easy to take care of.**

Note: **Use *that* or *which* for things.**

Notice that the verb in this type of adjective clause refers back to the word it modifies:

houses which are

furniture that is

Practice

Make sentences with adjective clauses introduced by *which* or *that*. Begin your sentences with *I like*.

1. houses I like houses which are easy to clean.
2. furniture ______
3. cities ______
4. architecture ______
5. clothes ______
6. food ______
7. cars ______
8. entertainment ______
9. books ______
10. music ______

Make It Work

Name three things you don't like. Use *which* or *that* in your sentences.

______

______

______

______

I like waiters who are pleasant.

ESSENTIAL ADJECTIVE CLAUSES: *WHO* VS. *WHICH*
SIMPLE PRESENT

GrammarGuide
3.7
7.10

I like restaurants [which] have good service.

I like waiters [who] are pleasant.

Note: Use *who* to introduce adjective clauses about people; use *which* to introduce adjective clauses about things.

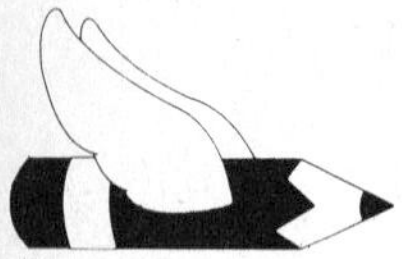

Practice

Make sentences with adjective clauses introduced by *who* or *which.* In order to practice *who* or *which*, do not use *that* in your sentences.

1. restaurants — I like restaurants which have good service.
2. food ______
3. waiters ______
4. salesclerks ______
5. department stores ______
6. movies ______
7. movie stars ______
8. singers ______
9. music ______
10. classes ______
11. teachers ______
12. apartment buildings ______
13. landlords ______
14. sports events ______
15. athletes ______

I think you work very hard.

ADVERBS OF MANNER

SIMPLE PRESENT

GrammarGuide **8.5**

I'm not a very graceful dancer.

I think you dance very **gracefully.**

Note: Add *ly* to form most adverbs of manner.
***Fast* and *hard* have the same form as the adjective.**

Irregular Form: good–well

Practice

Make sentences with adverbs.

1. I'm not a very good piano player. I think you play the piano very well.
2. I'm not a very quick learner. ______________________
3. I'm not a very cautious driver. ______________________
4. I'm not a very fast reader. ______________________
5. I'm not a very neat dresser. ______________________
6. I'm not a very graceful dancer. ______________________
7. I'm not a very good tennis player. ______________________
8. I'm not a very attentive listener. ______________________
9. I'm not a very hard worker. ______________________
10. I'm not a very fluent English speaker. ______________________

Make It Work

Fill in the dialogue.

■ Please sing a song for us.

□ I couldn't. I'm not a very good singer.

■ Oh, come on. ______________________________.

□ All right. I'll sing something for you.

I'm not a very good piano player. I can't play the piano very well.

ADJECTIVE VS. ADVERB

SIMPLE PRESENT, SIMPLE PAST

GrammarGuide
7.1
8.1

You play tennis very [well.]
You're a [good] tennis player.

Practice

Fill in the dialogues with either an adjective or an adverb.

■ Would you play the piano for us?

□ Oh, I can't play the piano very ____well____ .
(1. good/well)

■ Yes, you can. You play ________________ .
(2. beautiful/beautifully)

■ Would you sing a song with us?

□ I have a ________________ voice.
(3. terrible/terribly)

■ What do you mean? You sing very ________________ .
(4. good/well)

■ Dance with me.

□ I can't. I don't know how to dance.

■ That's not true. You're a ________________ dancer.
(5. good/well)

□ Do you really think so? I always thought I danced ________________ .
(6. bad/badly)

■ Tell us a joke. You tell jokes so ________________ .
(7. good/well)

□ That's not true. You're just a ________________ listener.
(8. good/well)

■ I'm sorry the house is so messy. I'm not a very ________________
(9. neat/neatly)
housekeeper.

□ Your house is always ________________ .
(10. immaculate/immaculately)

New Word:
immaculate–very clean

He should have practiced longer.

ADVERB COMPARATIVES

SHOULD HAVE

GrammarGuide
8.8

Did he run fast enough?

No. He should have run **faster.**

Did he play skillfully enough?

No. He should have played **more skillfully.**

Note: To form the comparative, add *-r* or *-er* to one-syllable adverbs. Put *more* before adverbs with two or more syllables.

Irregular Comparative Form: well–better
Irregular Past Participles:
hit–hit run–run go–gone

Practice

Make sentences with *should have* and the correct comparative form.

1. Did he practice for the tennis match long enough? — No. He should have practiced for the tennis match longer.
2. Did he hit the ball hard enough?
3. Did he hit the ball carefully enough?
4. Did he serve accurately enough?
5. Did he go to the net quickly enough?
6. Did he run fast enough?
7. Did he go to the net frequently enough?
8. Did he play skillfully enough?
9. Did he concentrate hard enough?
10. Did he play well enough?

New Words:

serve 

net 

match–a game where people compete
concentrate–have complete attention

Because Ruby works hard, she deserves a promotion.

ADVERBIAL CLAUSES WITH *BECAUSE* AND *ALTHOUGH*
SIMPLE PRESENT, FUTURE WITH *GOING TO*, PRESENT PERFECT

GrammarGuide
8.13

Because Irma has been with the company for many years, she deserves a promotion.

Although Irma has been with the company for many years, she doesn't deserve a promotion.

Note: Words like *because* and *since* show result; *although* and *even though* show contrast.

Punctuation: ***Although*** ______ [,] ______. ***Because*** ______ [,] ______.

Practice

Combine the sentences with *because* or *although.*

1. Irma has been with the company for many years. She doesn't deserve a promotion.
   Although Irma has been with the company for many years, she doesn't deserve a promotion.
2. Ruby hasn't been with the company for very long. She deserves a promotion.
   ______
3. Ruby works hard. She deserves a promotion.
   ______
4. Irma doesn't work hard. She doesn't deserve a promotion.
   ______
5. Irma always gets to work on time. She doesn't finish her work on time.
   ______
6. Ruby is sometimes late to work. She always finishes her work.
   ______
7. Ruby always finishes her work. She deserves a promotion.
   ______
8. Irma is a very good typist. She can't take shorthand.
   ______
9. Ruby is a good typist and can take shorthand. She deserves a promotion.
   ______
10. Ruby is the best employee. She's going to get a promotion.
   ______

I hope she has a boy.

CLAUSES WITH *HOPE*
AFFIRMATIVE STATEMENTS

GrammarGuide
6.5

Do you think Teresa will have a boy?

I | hope | she | has | a boy.

I hope that she has a boy.

Note: Use *hope* to express a desire that is expected to be fulfilled now or in the future.

The word *that* is optional.

Practice

Make sentences with *I hope*. Use pronouns in your sentences.

1. Do you think Teresa will have a boy? I hope she has a boy.
2. Do you think I'll pass the examination? I hope you pass the examination.
3. Do you think Dennis and Mako will get married? ____________
4. Do you think Sylvia will get a promotion? ____________
5. Do you think Nick Andropolis will win the election? ____________
6. Do you think Irving and Sally will get engaged? ____________
7. Do you think Victor will receive an award? ____________
8. Do you think I'll get a raise? ____________
9. Do you think Paul will graduate from law school? ____________
10. Do you think Andrea will be accepted to medical school? ____________

Make It Work

Name three things you hope for now or in the future.

____

____

____

New Word:
award–prize

I wish I didn't have to work.

CLAUSES WITH *WISH*: PRESENT EVENTS
NEGATIVE AND AFFIRMATIVE STATEMENTS

GrammarGuide **6.5**

He doesn't have to work.	**I**	**wish**	**I**	**didn't have**	**to work.**
He's independent.	**I**	**wish**	**I**	**were**	**independent.**

Note: Use *wish* + the past tense to express a desire that is not likely to be fulfilled now or in the future.
With the verb *to be*, use *were* for all persons.

The word *that* is optional.

Practice

Make sentences about yourself using *I wish.*

1. Simon doesn't have a care in the world. — I wish I didn't have a care in the world.
2. He doesn't have to worry about money. ____________
3. He doesn't have to buy clothes. ____________
4. He has a beautiful fur coat. ____________
5. He lives in a big house. ____________
6. He's independent. ____________
7. He doesn't have to work. ____________
8. He can sleep until noon every day. ____________
9. He doesn't have to be anywhere at any particular time. ____________
10. Simon is a cat. ____________

Make It Work

Make three wishes about your life now.

____

____

____

She wishes the guests hadn't arrived early.

CLAUSES WITH *WISH*: PAST EVENTS
NEGATIVE AND AFFIRMATIVE STATEMENTS

GrammarGuide **6.5**

The guests arrived early. Margo [wishes] the guests [hadn't] [arrived] early.

She wasn't ready. She [wishes] she [had been] ready.

Note: Use *wish* + the past perfect tense to express a desire that did not happen in the past.

Irregular Past Participle: forget–forgotten

Practice

Make sentences with *wish*.

1. The guests arrived early. — Margo wishes the guests hadn't arrived early.
2. She wasn't ready. — ______
3. She didn't have time to set the table in advance. — ______
4. She forgot to serve the appetizer. — ______
5. The roast wasn't done on time. — ______
6. She burned the potatoes. — ______
7. She spilled wine all over the table. — ______
8. The dessert didn't turn out. — ______
9. She wasn't able to spend time with her guests. — ______
10. The evening was a disaster! — ______

Make It Work

Write about an unpleasant event that happened to you in the past. Then make a wish about that event.

I lost my wedding ring. — I wish I hadn't lost it.

______ — ______

New Word:
appetizer–something that is eaten before or at the beginning of a meal

Her mother said that she was too young to get married.

Barbara is 17 years old. She wants to get married next month. Below are some comments about her plans to get married.

Her mother said to her, "You're too young to get married."
Her father said, "You can't get married until you're 18."
Her brother said, "You're making a big mistake."
Her sister said, "Your boyfriend isn't good enough for you."
The minister said, "You can't get married without your parents' consent."
The judge said, "You need your parents' consent."
Her grandmother said to her, "You're being very foolish."
Her uncle said, "You'll be sorry later."
Her aunt said to her, "You haven't known him long enough."
Her grandfather said, "Your boyfriend won't be able to support you."

New Words:
consent–permission
foolish–not wise, without good sense

Her mother said that she was too young to get married.

INDIRECT SPEECH: NOUN CLAUSES FROM STATEMENTS

GrammarGuide
6.5

Her uncle said to her, "You'll be sorry later."

Her uncle said that [she'd be] sorry later.

Her father said, "You can't get married until you're 18."

Her father said that [she couldn't get] married until [she was] 18.

Note: **When you report another person's words, change the pronouns as well as the verb tense.**

will **→** ***would***
can **→** ***could***
present tense → past tense
present perfect tense → past perfect tense

Practice

Below is a letter to the newspaper from Barbara's friend. Look at page 90. Then make sentences with indirect speech. Use pronouns to refer to *Barbara* (she, her, etc.).

Dear Abby,

My friend Barbara wants to get married. She is 17 years old, and she is still in high school. (1.) Her mother said that she was too young to get married. (2.) Her father said that ______________________. (3.) Even her sister said that ______________________. (4.) Her brother said that ______________________. (5.) Her grandmother said that ______________________. (6.) Her uncle said that ______________________. (7.) Her aunt said that ______________________. (8.) Her grandfather said that ______________________. (9.) She needs her parents' consent, and the minister said that ______________________. (10.) Even the judge said that ______________________.

She loves her boyfriend, and she wants to get married now. Can you tell me what I should say to Barbara?

Sincerely yours,
Barbara's friend

His uncle told him not to get married now.

INDIRECT SPEECH: INFINITIVE PHRASES FROM IMPERATIVES

GrammarGuide **6.5**

His mother said to him, "Wait until you're older."

His mother [told] [him to wait] until he was older.

His uncle said to him, "Don't get married now."

His uncle [told] [him not to get] married now.

Note: Use *told* with an indirect object without *to.*

Negatives are formed by placing *not* before the infinitive.

Practice

Barbara's boyfriend is only 18 years old. He has just graduated from high school. He loves Barbara, and he wants to get married. Below are some comments about his plans to get married.

Change the direct speech to indirect speech, and change *say* to *tell.*

1. His mother said to him, "Wait until you're older." — His mother told him to wait until he was older.
2. His father said to him, "Don't get married until you have a job." ______
3. The minister said to him, "Don't rush into marriage." ______
4. His grandfather said to him, "Enjoy yourself while you're young." ______
5. His best friend said to him, "Do what you think is right." ______
6. Another friend said to him, "Try to forget Barbara." ______
7. Barbara's father said to him, "Wait until Barbara is 18." ______
8. His sister said to him, "Don't get married until you're 21." ______
9. His high school teacher said to him, "Get a college education first." ______
10. His brother said to him, "Get to know Barbara better before you marry her." ______

The interviewer asked Diane if she could begin tomorrow.

INDIRECT SPEECH: NOUN CLAUSES FROM YES-NO QUESTIONS

GrammarGuide **6.5**

The interviewer asked Diane, "Can you begin tomorrow?"

The interviewer asked Diane [if] [she] [could begin] tomorrow.

Note: Use *if* (or *whether*) with yes-no questions in indirect speech. Notice that question word order changes to statement word order.

Remember to change present tense to past tense, *can* to *could*, and *will* to *would*.

Practice

Change the direct questions to indirect questions.

1. "Can you speak Spanish?" the interviewer asked Diane. — The interviewer asked Diane if she could speak Spanish.
2. "Can you type?" he asked Diane. ______________________________
3. "Do you have any office experience?" he asked Diane. ______________________________
4. He asked Diane, "Will you work overtime?" ______________________________
5. "Are you a high school graduate?" he asked her. ______________________________
6. "Will you work at night?" he asked her. ______________________________
7. "Can you take shorthand?" the interviewer asked her. ______________________________
8. He asked, "Are you a college graduate?" ______________________________
9. "Will you work on Saturdays?" the interviewer asked. ______________________________
10. The interviewer asked Diane, "Can you begin tomorrow?" ______________________________

The interviewer asked Diane how fast she could type.

INDIRECT SPEECH: NOUN CLAUSES FROM INFORMATION QUESTIONS

GrammarGuide
6.5

The interviewer asked Diane, "How fast can you type?"

The interviewer asked Diane | **how fast** | **she** | **could type.** |

Note: Notice that question word order changes to statement word order.

Remember to change present tense to past tense, past and present perfect to past perfect, *can* to *could,* and *will* to *would.*

In informal speech, the past tense is sometimes used in place of the past perfect tense.

Practice

Change the direct questions to indirect questions.

1. The interviewer asked Diane, "Where do you live?" The interviewer asked Diane where she lived.
2. He asked Diane, "How many languages can you speak?" ______
3. The interviewer asked Diane, "How fast can you type?" ______
4. "What college did you graduate from?" he asked Diane. ______
5. He asked her, "When did you graduate from high school?" ______
6. He asked her, "How much office experience have you had?" ______
7. "How long did you work for Selby Company?" he asked her. ______
8. "How fast can you take shorthand?" he asked Diane. ______
9. He asked Diane, "Why do you want to work for A.B.C. Company?" ______
10. "When can you begin work?" he asked her. ______

I can't believe he asked her if she was happily married.

INDIRECT SPEECH: NOUN CLAUSES FROM YES-NO QUESTIONS AND INFORMATION QUESTIONS

GrammarGuide **6.5**

The interviewer asked Diane, "Are you happily married?"

I can't believe the interviewer asked Diane [if] [she] [was] happily married.

He asked her, "Why don't you have any children?"

I can't believe he asked her [why] [she] [didn't have] any children.

Note: Use *if* (or *whether*) with yes-no questions in indirect speech.

Notice that question word order changes to statement word order.

Practice

Here are some personal questions the interviewer asked Diane. Change the direct questions to indirect questions. Begin each indirect question with *I can't believe.*

1. He asked her, "Are you married?" — I can't believe he asked her if she was married.
2. He asked her, "Are you happily married?" ______
3. He asked her, "Do you have any children?" ______
4. "Why don't you have any children?" he asked her. ______
5. He asked her, "Are you planning on having a family?" ______
6. "How much money does your husband make?" he asked her. ______
7. He asked her, "How old are you?" ______
8. "What religion are you?" he asked her. ______
9. He asked her, "What political party do you belong to?" ______
10. He asked her, "Do you have any personal problems?" ______

New Word:
party–group or association

He was Sales Manager for four years.

FOR, SINCE,* AND *AGO

SIMPLE PAST, PRESENT PERFECT

GrammarGuide
8.3
9.3

Julia started working at Selby Company five years [ago.]

She's been working there [for] five years.

She's been working there [since] 1978.

Note: Use *since* with a beginning time.

Use *for* and *ago* with a period of time. Notice that the order is reversed:
for five years five years ago

Practice

Fill in the blanks with *for, since,* or *ago.*

1. Fernando started working at Selby Company eight years ____ago____ .
2. He's been working there ____________ 1975.
3. ____________ three years, Fernando worked as Assistant Sales Manager.
4. Then, five years ____________, he became Sales Manager.
5. He was Sales Manager ____________ four years.
6. He was promoted to Vice-President ten months ____________.
7. He's been Vice-President ____________ last March.
8. Julia has also been working at Selby Company, but she's only been working there ____________ 1978.
9. She's been working there ____________ five years.
10. ____________ a year, she worked as a secretary in the Sales Department.
11. Four years ____________, she was promoted to Assistant Sales Manager.
12. She was Assistant Sales Manager ____________ three years.
13. Eight months ____________, after Fernando became Vice-President, Julia was promoted to Sales Manager.
14. She's had this position ____________ last May.
15. She's been Sales Manager ____________ about eight months.

Make It Work

Tell about your job. Tell about when you started working, how long you've been there, and any promotions you have had.

____

____

____

She bought gifts for her family.

_TO_ OR _FOR_ VS. NO PREPOSITION

SIMPLE PAST

GrammarGuide **9.4**

	Objects			
	indirect	***direct***		***indirect***
She served	**her family**	**turkey.**		
She served		**turkey**	**to**	**her family.**

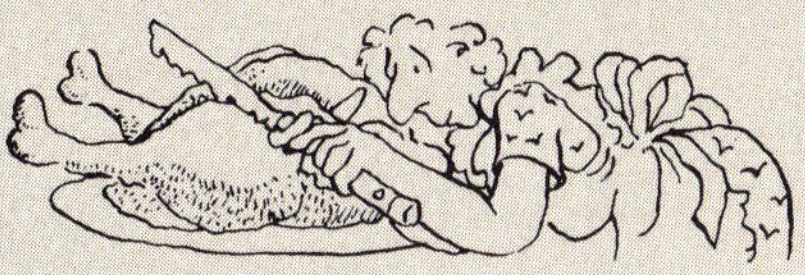

Note: **Use *to* or *for* when the indirect object comes after the direct object. Do not use *to* or *for* when the indirect object comes first.**

Use *to* with these verbs:
send mail read give serve

Use *for* with these verbs:
buy get cook order make bake

Practice

Fill in the blanks with *to, for,* or a line for nothing (---).

1. Beatrice sent holiday cards __to__ her friends.
2. She mailed ______ her grandmother a gift.
3. She also mailed a gift ______ her aunt overseas.
4. She bought gifts ______ her family.
5. She got toys ______ her children.
6. She also bought ______ them some candy.
7. She gave a book ______ her father.
8. She ordered ______ her mother some flowers.
9. She made an apron ______ her sister.
10. She baked some cookies ______ her aunt and uncle.
11. She got ______ her husband a tie.
12. She cooked a big meal ______ her family.
13. She served ______ everyone turkey.
14. For dessert, she served pumpkin pie ______ everyone.
15. She read a holiday story ______ her children.

Make It Work

Name three things you did last holiday season.

I sent ____.

I bought ____.

____.

He'll stay in Quito from Monday to Wednesday.

GrammarGuide
9.2
9.3

Time		Place	
in	1983 January the winter the evening the afternoon the morning	in	Quito Ecuador the center of town
on	Tuesday Wednesday night January 20th the evening of January 20th	on	Tenth Street Seventh Avenue
at	6:00 noon, night, midnight	at	47-16 Tenth Street
from	5:00 to (or until) 6:00	from	Lima to Cuzco

Note: Use *in* with months, seasons, and years.

Use *on* with days.

Use *at* with the time of day.

Use *from–to* (or *until*) with a beginning time (or day) and an end time (or day).

Use *in* for cities and countries.

Use *on* with street names.

Use *at* with addresses.

Use *from–to* with a beginning point and an end point.

He'll stay in Quito from Monday to Wednesday.

PREPOSITIONS OF TIME AND PLACE

FUTURE WITH *WILL*

Practice

Ken is going to South America for a week. Here are his plans for his trip. Look at page 98. Then fill in the blanks with *in, on, at,* or *from–to*.

1. He'll travel to South America ___in___ January, when it's warm and pleasant.
2. He'll arrive ________ Bogotá, Colombia, ________ Saturday, January 16th.
3. He'll arrive ________ 6:00 ________ the morning.
4. He'll stay at the Tequendama Hotel, located ________ 10-42 Twenty-sixth Street.
5. ________ Sunday, he'll visit the National Museum ________ Seventh Avenue.
6. He'll fly ________ Bogotá ________ Quito, Ecuador, the next day.
7. When he's ________ Quito, he'll visit a lot of beautiful cathedrals.
8. He'll stay in Quito ________ Monday ________ Wednesday.
9. ________ Wednesday evening, he'll fly to Lima, Peru.
10. He'll stay ________ the modern part of the city.
11. ________ the morning ________ Thursday, he'll visit the National Museum of Art.
12. ________ noon, he'll take a plane to the city of Cuzco, where he'll spend the night.
13. The next morning ________ exactly 7:10, he'll take a train ________ Cuzco ________ Machu-Picchu.
14. He'll spend the night ________ Machu-Picchu.
15. ________ the morning of January 23rd, he'll fly ________ Machu-Picchu ________ Lima. From Lima, he'll take a plane back to the United States.

Make It Work

You are going to take a vacation for a week. Tell where you'll go, when you'll leave and return, where you'll stay, and what you plan to see.

____

____

____

____

Everyone laughed at his joke.

VERB + PREPOSITION
SIMPLE PAST, PAST CONTINUOUS

GrammarGuide
9.9

at	about (or of)	for	to
look	think	wait	listen
glance	talk	watch	pay attention
laugh	speak	look	talk
smile			speak

Note: Some verbs occur with more than one preposition:

look at (something or someone)–watch (something or someone)
look for–try to find

talk to someone–*someone* is the listener
talk about something–*something* is the subject of the talk

Practice

Fill in the blanks with *at, about, for,* or *to.*

1. The man stepped onto the platform and smiled ___at___ the crowd.
2. Then he looked ________ the crowd.
3. He took the microphone and spoke ________ the crowd.
4. The people listened ________ him very carefully.
5. They thought ________ his ideas.
6. They were looking ________ answers to their problems.
7. The man talked ________ the problems in the country, but he didn't say very much.
8. He told a joke, and then he waited ________ the crowd to laugh.
9. Everyone laughed ________ his joke.
10. A woman from the crowd asked a question, but he didn't pay any attention ________ her.
11. He quickly glanced ________ his watch.
12. He waited ________ his limousine to drive up. Then the politician waved to the crowd and drove off in his limousine.

New Words:
limousine–a car with the driver's seat separated from the back

platform  **microphone** 

Carla is nervous about taking the exam.

VERB FORMS AFTER PREPOSITIONS

SIMPLE PRESENT, FUTURE WITH *WILL*

GrammarGuide **6.4**

Carla is nervous about [taking] the exam.

She's afraid of [not passing] it.

Note: Use the verb + *ing* after a preposition.
Negatives are formed by placing *not* before the verb.

Practice

Carla is going to take a math exam next week. She needs to pass the exam in order to get a high school diploma.

Fill in the blanks with the correct form of the verb.

1. (take) It's a three-hour exam, and she's very nervous about taking it.
2. (figure/take) She's good at ____________ out math problems, but she's bad at ____________ exams.
3. (select) She's never sure of ____________ the correct answer.
4. (not/make) She always changes her mind and worries about ____________ the correct choice.
5. (guess) She's not very lucky at ____________ the correct answer either.
6. (not/pass) Her problem is that she's afraid of ____________ an exam.
7. (fail) She's concerned about ____________ before she's even taken the exam.
8. (do) The day of the exam, she'll be nervous about ____________ her best.
9. (take) After it's over, she'll dream about ____________ the exam.
10. (not/do) If she doesn't get a high score, she'll be ashamed of ____________ better. If she does well on the exam, she'll say she was lucky.

Make It Work

Answer the questions.

Are you nervous or calm about taking exams? ____________________

Are you good or bad at taking exams? ____________________

Are you lucky or unlucky at guessing the correct answer? ____________________

If you get a passing score on your exam, do you feel happy about passing or do you feel sorry about not doing better? ____________________

I'm good at tennis.

ADJECTIVE + PREPOSITION

SIMPLE PRESENT

GrammarGuide **7.12**

interested disappointed | **in** |

tired afraid ashamed sure certain jealous | **of** |

concerned worried nervous excited happy glad sure certain | **about** |

bored disappointed | **with** |

good bad slow lucky surprised angry | **at** |

Note: Some adjectives occur with more than one preposition without changing meaning:
sure of sure about
disappointed in disappointed with

Practice

Fill in the blanks with the correct preposition. Then answer the questions. Tell about yourself.

1. What kind of television shows are you interested __in__ ? I'm interested in talk shows.
2. What kind of television shows are you bored ____ ? ____________________
3. What sports are you good ____ ? ____________________
4. What animals are you afraid ____ ? ____________________
5. What games are you unlucky ____ ? ____________________
6. What kind of activities are you tired ____ ? ____________________
7. What problem are you worried ____ ? ____________________
8. What event in your life are you happy ____ ? ____________________
9. Who are you jealous ____ ? ____________________
10. Who are you angry ____ ? ____________________

I am interested in renting a room.

VERB COMPLEMENTS

SIMPLE PRESENT, FUTURE WITH *WILL*

GrammarGuide **6.4**

I am interested in [renting] a room.

I would like to [move] in on September 1st.

Note: Use the *ing* form of the verb after prepositions:

interested in renting   look forward to seeing   worried about renting

Do not use the *ing* form with verb + infinitive combinations:

have to find   want to see   expect to pay   used to live

Practice

Fill in the blanks with the correct form of the verb.

Dear Sir or Madam:

I am replying to your advertisement in the *Gazette* for a furnished room. I plan on ___studying___ (1. study) at the university this fall, and I am interested in __________ (2. find) a room near the campus. I expect to __________ (3. start) school on September 15th and would probably need to __________ (4. move) in around the first week of September. I want to __________ (5. rent) a single room with a private bath if possible. I am interested in __________ (6. spend) between $70.00 and $90.00 a week.

I do not have any references because I have always lived at home. If you are concerned about __________ (7. obtain) a reference, I can get a reference from a former employer. I used to __________ (8. work) at Blue Bell Nursery in Los Angeles.

I will be in Berkeley on August 18th. I would like to __________ (9. see) the apartment when I am there. I look forward to __________ (10. hear) from you.

Sincerely yours,

Yoichi Watanabe

Yoichi Watanabe

New Words:
furnished–with furniture
references–written information about someone's character
obtain–get
former–past

Do you want me to type it up today?

SEPARABLE TWO-WORD VERBS

SIMPLE PRESENT

GrammarGuide **6.3**

	Hand		**out**	**copies to everyone.**
	Hand	**copies**	**out**	**to everyone.**
Do you want me to	**hand**	**them**	**out**	**to everyone today?**

Note: When the direct object is a noun, it can come before or after the particle. When the direct object is a pronoun, it comes before the particle.

Common particles: in out over off on up down

Practice

Make questions with direct object pronouns. Begin your questions with *Do you want me to.*

1. Do over the sales report. Do you want me to do it over today?
2. Fill in the chart. ______
3. Look up the information in the annual report. ______
4. Add up the figures. ______
5. Write down the total. ______
6. Type up the report. ______
7. Run off fifty copies. ______
8. Hand out copies to all the salespeople. ______
9. Call up Mr. Suzuki. ______
10. Turn in the original copy to Mr. Suzuki. ______

New Words:
do over–do again
run off–duplicate
hand out–distribute
annual–yearly

Answers to Exercises

Page 1

2. Radishes and onions are vegetables.
3. Strawberries and raspberries are fruits.
4. Potatoes and carrots are vegetables.
5. Irises and pansies are flowers.
6. Apples and cherries are fruits.
7. Lilies and orchids are flowers.
8. Cucumbers and tomatoes are vegetables.
9. Plums and peaches are fruits.

Page 2

2. lot
3. trees
4. story
5. stories
6. rooms
7. things
8. rooms
9. dishwasher
10. cabinets
11. bathrooms
12. bath
13. baths
14. months

Page 3

2. Could they be Susan Abbott's?
3. Could they be David Barnes'?
4. Could they be David's girlfriend's?
5. Could they be the Kotches'?
6. Could they be Susie Kirby's?
7. Could they be Doris Gross'?
8. Could they be Harry Schwartz's?
9. Could they be Harry's friends'?
10. Could they be Alex Dunn's?
11. Could they be the Davises'?
12. Could they be Jack Davis' brother's?

Page 4

3. ---
4. ---
5. best-sellers
6. biographies
7. ---
8. ---
9. dictionaries
10. ---
11. ---
12. ---
13. hobbies
14. indoor games
15. ---
16. ---
17. mysteries
18. pets
19. ---
20. ---

Page 5

Individual answers. Some suggested answers are:

3. more (less)
4. more
5. fewer
6. more
7. less
8. fewer
9. more
10. less
11. more
12. less
13. less (more)
14. more
15. fewer

Page 7

3. the fewest
4. the most
5. the fewest
6. fewer
7. the most
8. the fewest
9. more
10. fewer
11. less
12. the least
13. less
14. the most
15. the most

Page 8

2. an
3. a
4. a
5. an
6. a
7. an
8. an
9. a
10. an
11. an
12. a
13. an
14. a
15. an
16. a
17. a
18. a
19. an
20. an
21. a
22. an
23. a
24. a
25. an
26. an
27. a
28. a
29. an
30. a

Page 9

2. Are you a registered plumber?
3. Are you an authorized Ford dealer?
4. Are you a licensed pharmacist?
5. Are you a registered nurse?
6. Are you a certified public accountant?
7. Are you an insured savings bank?
8. Are you a licensed day care center?
9. Are you an accredited computer school?
10. Are you an authorized Evinrude dealer?

Page 10

Some suggested answers are:

3. furniture
4. a floor
5. a shirt
6. a coat
7. a tie
8. a bow
9. pizza
10. bread
11. a newspaper
12. mail
13. a grape
14. a cherry
15. gasoline
16. paint
17. an elephant
18. a horse
19. a typewriter
20. an adding machine

Page 11

2. a/a
3. the/the
4. a/a
5. the
6. the/the
7. the/the
8. the/the/the
9. the
10. the/the

Pages 12 and 13

2. ---
3. The
4. a
5. ---
6. ---
7. an
8. The
9. ---/---/---/---/---/---
10. a/---
11. The/the
12. ---
13. ---
14. a
15. The
16. ---
17. The
18. a
19. a
20. the

Page 14

2. some
3. a
4. some
5. a
6. some
7. a
8. some
9. some
10. a
11. some
12. some
13. a
14. an
15. some

Page 15

2. ---/the
3. ---/the
4. the/the
5. ---
6. the/---
7. ---/the
8. ---
9. the
10. the
11. ---
12. the

Page 17

3. the/---
4. ---/the
5. ---
6. ---/---
7. the/---
8. the/the
9. ---
10. ---/---
11. the
12. ---
13. ---
14. ---
15. ---/---

Page 18

2. themselves
3. ourselves
4. himself
5. myself
6. yourself
7. yourself
8. herself
9. herself
10. myself
11. yourself
12. ourselves

Page 19

2. The other
3. The others
4. The other
5. Another
6. Another
7. The other
8. The others
9. Another
10. The others

Page 20

2. anyone
3. no one
4. nothing
5. nothing
6. someone
7. someone
8. anyone
9. someone
10. anything

Make It Work

someone
No one
Nothing
No one

Page 21

2. Who's
3. Who's
4. whose
5. Whose
6. Whose
7. Whose
8. Who's
9. who's
10. Whose
11. Who's
12. Who's

Page 22

2. They're
3. They're
4. their
5. Their
6. there
7. their
8. there
9. there
10. their
11. There
12. their
13. there
14. their
15. they're

Page 23

Individual answers beginning with:

3. Rent costs me . . .
4. Gas costs me . . .
5. Electricity costs me . . .
6. Water costs me . . .
7. Car payments cost me . . .
8. Gas for the car costs me . . .
9. Food costs me . . .
10. Medicine costs me . . .
11. Haircuts cost me . . .
12. Dry cleaning costs me . . .
13. Telephone bills cost me . . .
14. Clothes cost me . . .
15. Entertainment costs me . . .

Page 24

Individual answers.

Page 25

Individual answers.

Page 26

2. works
3. takes
4. studies
5. have
6. has
7. goes
8. get
9. gets
10. lasts
11. practices
12. loves

Page 27

2. There's
3. There are
4. There are
5. There are
6. There are
7. There are
8. There are
9. There's
10. There are
11. There's
12. There's
13. There's
14. There's
15. There are

Pages 28 and 29

2. arrived
3. came
4. turned
5. said
6. knew
7. thought
8. stood
9. got
10. happened
11. met
12. asked
13. mentioned
14. understood
15. explained
16. told
17. decided
18. walked
19. said
20. smiled

Pages 30 and 31

2. grew
3. went
4. read
5. had
6. said
7. spent
8. was
9. decided
10. wanted
11. wrote
12. rejected
13. published
14. was
15. thought
16. said
17. came
18. wrote
19. became
20. confessed

Page 32

2. grew
3. go
4. tutored
5. read
6. make
7. challenged
8. accept
9. completed
10. publish
11. rejected
12. had
13. have
14. thought
15. think

Page 33

Individual answers.

Page 34

2. He'll sail from Puerto Rico to St. Thomas on December 1.
3. He's going to stop in Antigua on December 3.
4. He'll stop in Antigua on December 3.
5. He's going to visit Martinique on December 5.
6. He'll visit Martinique on December 5.
7. He's going to see Trinidad on December 8.
8. He'll see Trinidad on December 8.
9. He's going to stay in Caracas on December 9 and 10.
10. He'll stay in Caracas on December 9 and 10.
11. He's going to fly back to Puerto Rico on December 11.
12. He'll fly back to Puerto Rico on December 11.

Page 35

2. 'll go/sees
3. 'll do/'s
4. visits/'ll go
5. arrives/'ll go
6. 'll buy
7. won't go/leaves
8. 'll go
9. 's, 'll visit
10. won't have

Page 37

2. are sitting
3. are getting (are trying to get)
4. is pushing
5. is holding (is carrying)
6. is eating
7. is reading
8. is sleeping
9. is stealing (is taking)
10. are listening
11. is sitting
12. is smoking

Page 38

2. was depositing
3. were standing
4. were talking
5. was writing
6. was endorsing
7. were filling
8. was sitting
9. were applying
10. were waiting

Make It Work

Page 39

2. was taking/rang
3. were having/arrived
4. rang/was talking
5. was talking/started
6. was feeding/had
7. were playing/started
8. was eating/began
9. decided
10. was watching/came

Page 40

3. Louis won't be coming (to the party).
4. Pat and Cathy will be coming.
5. Mary will be coming.
6. Paul and Laura will be coming.
7. Tish will be coming with Paul and Laura.
8. David will be bringing a guest.
9. Gary will probably be arriving late.
10. John and his wife won't be coming.

Make It Work

11 people

David will be bringing a guest.

Page 41

2. You mean she's been watering the lawn for four hours?
3. You mean they've been pulling weeds for an hour?
4. You mean she's been planting flowers for two hours?
5. You mean they've been painting the house for six hours?
6. You mean he's been putting up the storm windows for two hours?
7. You mean they've been washing the windows for four hours?
8. You mean he's been fixing the driveway for three hours?
9. You mean she's been sweeping the patio for an hour?
10. You mean he's been trimming the bushes for three hours?

Page 42

3. I've already chosen an English class.
4. I haven't made an appointment with the foreign student adviser yet.
5. I've already read the student handbook.
6. I haven't met the instructor yet.
7. I haven't spoken to the instructor yet.
8. I haven't gone to the bookstore yet. (I haven't been to the bookstore yet.)
9. I haven't bought a dictionary yet.
10. I've already done the homework.

Page 43

Individual answers.

Page 44

2. Have you ever spent Egyptian money?
3. Have you ever gone (been) to a bazaar?
4. Have you ever bought Egyptian jewelry?
5. Have you ever taken a boat trip up the Nile?
6. Have you ever ridden a camel?
7. Have you ever stood in front of a temple?
8. Have you ever seen the pyramids?
9. Have you ever read a book on the history of Egypt?
10. Have you ever gotten up at 4:30 to see a sunrise?
11. Have you ever worn a veil?
12. Have you ever brought home souvenirs of your trip?

Page 45

2. By the time Gary got there, the guests had arrived.
3. By the time Gary got there, the guests had met one another.
4. By the time Gary got there, everyone had eaten a piece of cake.
5. By the time Gary got there, everyone had had a glass of champagne.
6. By the time Gary got there, the band had started to play.
7. By the time Gary got there, the bride had danced with the groom.
8. By the time Gary got there, several people had left the reception.
9. By the time Gary got there, the bride had thrown the bouquet.
10. By the time Gary got there, the photographer had taken a lot of pictures.

Page 46

2. Until last week, he hadn't flown on a jet.
3. Until last week, he hadn't seen snow.
4. Until last week, he hadn't spoken English.
5. Until last week, he hadn't met an American.
6. Until last week, he hadn't eaten a hamburger.
7. Until last week, he hadn't drunk a milk shake.
8. Until last week, he hadn't seen pop art.
9. Until last week, he hadn't heard country music.
10. Until last week, he hadn't gone (been) to a barbecue.

Page 47

2. are
3. wore
4. carried
5. were
6. was
7. served
8. were
9. graduated
10. works
11. works
12. is ('s)
13. will attend
14. will major ('ll major)
15. will reside

Page 48

2. to have
3. retiring
4. working/to do
5. being
6. working
7. swimming/gardening
8. doing
9. writing/to take
10. to travel

Page 49

2. 's traveled
3. 've been
4. spent
5. flew
6. went
7. hired
8. saw
9. went
10. drove
11. visited
12. haven't been
13. have never traveled
14. 've never heard
15. has been

Page 51

3. No, it isn't.
4. No, it doesn't.
5. Yes, you will.
6. Yes, it will.
7. No, you don't.
8. Yes, you can.
9. Yes, it is.
10. No, it isn't.
11. No, there aren't.
12. No, they won't.
13. No, it isn't.
14. No, it isn't.
15. No, it isn't. (Yes, it is.)

Page 52

2. didn't she?
3. didn't she?
4. wasn't she?
5. isn't she?
6. didn't she?
7. hadn't she?
8. isn't she?
9. hasn't she?
10. won't you?

Page 53

2. If you visit our shop, you'll receive a free gift.
3. If you buy a new car now, you'll get a $250 rebate.
4. If you call this number now, you'll get a set of steak knives.
5. If you subscribe to *Now* magazine, you'll save 50% on the regular price.
6. If you fill in your name and birthdate, you'll receive a free necklace.
7. If you visit our pharmacy, you'll get $1.00 off on any prescription.
8. If you open a new account at Century Savings, you'll receive a free set of dishes.
9. If you buy three bars of soap, you'll get one absolutely free.
10. If you present this coupon at your grocery store, you'll save 50¢ on your next purchase of Homestyle Potato Chips.

Page 54

Individual answers beginning with: *If I were . . .*

Page 55

Individual answers.

Page 56

2. If I had been Thomas Becket, I would (wouldn't) have died for my country.
3. If I had been Susan B. Anthony, I would (wouldn't) have fought for women's rights.
4. If I had been King Henry VIII, I wouldn't (would) have had seven wives.
5. If I had been Jean-Paul Sartre, I wouldn't (would) have refused the Nobel Prize.
6. If I had been King Edward of England, I wouldn't (would) have given up my throne for a woman.
7. If I had been Joan of Arc, I would (wouldn't) have died for my country.
8. If I had been Martin Luther King, I would (wouldn't) have fought for civil rights.

Page 57

2. If she hadn't been in a hurry, she wouldn't have had to run to the train station.
3. If she hadn't had to run to the train station, she wouldn't have slipped on the ice.
4. If she hadn't slipped on the ice, her briefcase wouldn't have flown open.
5. If her briefcase hadn't flown open, her papers wouldn't have been scattered everywhere.
6. If her papers hadn't been scattered everywhere, she wouldn't have had to pick them up.
7. If she hadn't had to pick them up, she wouldn't have arrived at the train station late.
8. If she hadn't arrived at the train station late, she wouldn't have missed her train.
9. If she hadn't missed her train, she wouldn't have arrived at the office late.
10. If she hadn't arrived at the office late, her boss wouldn't have been angry.

Page 58

Individual answers. Suggested answers are:

2. I should do the laundry, but I'd rather go to the movies.
3. I should clean the house, but I'd rather watch the baseball game.
4. I should mow the lawn, but I'd rather take a nap.
5. I should fix dinner, but I'd rather go out.
6. I should get up early, but I'd rather stay in bed.
7. I should drink a glass of milk, but I'd rather have some soda.
8. I should do the dishes, but I'd rather watch television.
9. I should go to work, but I'd rather stay home.
10. I should do my work, but I'd rather go to the party.

Page 59

2. have to
3. don't have to
4. have to
5. must not
6. have to
7. must not
8. don't have to
9. must not
10. have to

Page 60

Individual answers.

Page 61

Suggested answers:

3. It could be a hat.
4. It might be a hill.
5. It could be an M.
6. It might be two mountains.
7. It could be two birds.
8. It might be a mustache.
9. It could be a fried egg.
10. It might be a cup and saucer.

Page 62

2. used to work
3. used to live
4. used to spend
5. used to take
6. used to go
7. used to make
8. used to be
9. used to take
10. used to have

Page 63

2. isn't used to working
3. isn't used to commuting
4. isn't used to living
5. isn't used to living
6. isn't used to cooking
7. isn't used to cleaning
8. isn't used to doing
9. isn't used to supporting
10. isn't used to paying

Page 64

2. She should have turned off the lights.
3. She should have fed the dog.
4. She should have closed the windows.
5. She should have taken out the trash.
6. She should have made sure the oven was off.
7. She should have turned the radio off.
8. She should have locked all the doors.
9. She should have taken her keys with her.
10. She should have taken her money with her.

Page 65

2. She could have fallen off the ladder.
3. They could have caught a cold.
4. You could have hurt your back.
5. She could have had an accident.
6. He could have been hit by a car.
7. The children (They) could have shot someone.
8. They could have gotten hurt.
9. She could have gotten a shock.
10. The little boy (He) could have drowned.

Page 66

2. be
3. look
4. laid
5. be
6. remember
7. left
8. look
9. looked
10. taken
11. help
12. get
13. stay
14. make
15. find

Page 67

2. is known
3. are treated
4. is tastefully decorated
5. are located
6. is provided
7. are included
8. is limited
9. are required
10. are accepted

Page 68

2. wasn't built
3. was built
4. wasn't designed
5. was copied
6. wasn't used
7. was designed
8. wasn't painted
9. was removed
10. wasn't made
11. was made
12. was bought
13. were replaced
14. was remodeled
15. were replaced

Page 69

3. called
4. arrived
5. was rushed
6. examined
7. was taken
8. wasn't injured
9. was bruised
10. wasn't broken
11. told
12. was notified

Page 70

2. The meeting will be held at the Manor Hotel.
3. All salespeople will be expected to attend.
4. Transportation will be provided.
5. Sales will be discussed from 9:00 to 11:00.
6. A sales report will be given from 11:00 to 12:00.
7. Lunch will be eaten from 12:00 to 1:00.
8. The people will be divided into two groups from 2:00 to 4:00.
9. A cocktail party will be given at 5:00.
10. Dinner will be served at 8:00.

Page 71

Individual answers.

Pages 72 and 73

2. Air pollution comes from incinerators and smokestacks.
3. It also comes from automobiles, buses(,) and trucks.
4. Water pollution comes from chemical waste and trash.
5. People throw trash into our rivers, lakes(,) and oceans.
6. Factories dump chemical waste, oil(,) and detergents into our water.
7. Noise pollution comes from cars, car horns(,) and subways.
8. Also, construction work and loud radios can cause noise pollution.
9. Our world is becoming unhealthy for people and animals.
10. However, people, companies(,) and the government can do something about it.

Page 74

3. Yukiko can type, but she can't take shorthand.
4. She was pleasant and polite in the interview, but Mr. Simon isn't going to hire her.
5. She can't take shorthand, and she doesn't have any experience.
6. María can type, and she can take shorthand.
7. She didn't make a good impression in the interview, so Mr. Simon isn't going to hire her.
8. Carlos can take shorthand, and he can type.
9. He was pleasant and polite in the interview, and he has a lot of experience.
10. Carlos is the best person for the job, so Mr. Simon is going to offer the job to Carlos.

Page 75

Individual answers ending in:

2. ...funnier
3. ...more educational
4. ...more amusing
5. ...sillier
6. ...more informative
7. ...more interesting
8. ...more terrifying
9. ...more exciting
10. ...more popular

Pages 76 and 77

2. the largest
3. the mightiest
4. (the) most exotic
5. the most exciting
6. the biggest
7. the bravest
8. the tallest
9. (the) most spectacular
10. the prettiest
11. the most fantastic
12. the most delicious
13. the best
14. The most wonderful
15. the most expensive

Page 78

2. bored
3. exciting
4. disappointed
5. boring
6. exhausted
7. amazing
8. amazed
9. terrifying
10. entertaining

Page 79

2. any
3. any
4. no
5. none
6. any
7. any
8. none
9. any
10. None
11. any
12. no

Page 80

Individual answers.

Page 81

Individual answers.

Page 82

Individual answers.

Page 83

2. I think you learn very quickly.
3. I think you drive very cautiously.
4. I think you read very fast.
5. I think you dress very neatly.
6. I think you dance very gracefully.
7. I think you play tennis very well.
8. I think you listen very attentively.
9. I think you work very hard.
10. I think you speak English very fluently.

Page 84

2. beautifully
3. terrible
4. well
5. good
6. badly
7. well
8. good
9. neat
10. immaculate

Page 85

2. No. He should have hit the ball harder.
3. No. He should have hit the ball more carefully.
4. No. He should have served more accurately.
5. No. He should have gone to the net more quickly.
6. No. He should have run faster.
7. No. He should have gone to the net more frequently.
8. No. He should have played more skillfully.
9. No. He should have concentrated harder.
10. No. He should have played better.

Page 86

2. Although Ruby hasn't been with the company for very long, she deserves a promotion.
3. Because Ruby works hard, she deserves a promotion.
4. Because Irma doesn't work hard, she doesn't deserve a promotion.
5. Although Irma always gets to work on time, she doesn't finish her work on time.
6. Although Ruby is sometimes late to work, she always finishes her work.
7. Because Ruby always finishes her work, she deserves a promotion.
8. Although Irma is a very good typist, she can't take shorthand.
9. Because Ruby is a good typist and can take shorthand, she deserves a promotion.
10. Because Ruby is the best employee, she's going to get a promotion.

Page 87

3. I hope (that) they get married.
4. I hope (that) she gets a promotion.
5. I hope (that) he wins the election.
6. I hope (that) they get engaged.
7. I hope (that) he receives an award.
8. I hope (that) you get a raise.
9. I hope (that) he graduates from law school.
10. I hope (that) she's (she is) accepted to medical school.

Page 88

2. I wish (that) I didn't have to worry about money.
3. I wish (that) I didn't have to buy clothes.
4. I wish (that) I had a beautiful fur coat.
5. I wish (that) I lived in a big house.
6. I wish (that) I were independent.
7. I wish (that) I didn't have to work.
8. I wish (that) I could sleep until noon every day.
9. I wish (that) I didn't have to be anywhere at any particular time.
10. I wish (that) I were a cat.

Page 89

2. She wishes (that) she had been ready.
3. She wishes (that) she had had time to set the table in advance.
4. She wishes (that) she hadn't forgotten to serve the appetizer.
5. She wishes (that) the roast had been done on time.
6. She wishes (that) she hadn't burned the potatoes.
7. She wishes (that) she hadn't spilled wine all over the table.
8. She wishes (that) the dessert had turned out.
9. She wishes (that) she had been able to spend more time with her guests.
10. She wishes (that) the evening hadn't been a disaster.

Page 91

2. Her father said that she couldn't get married until she was 18.
3. Even her sister said that her boyfriend wasn't good enough for her.
4. Her brother said that she was making a big mistake.
5. Her grandmother said that she was being very foolish.
6. Her uncle said that she'd (she would) be sorry later.
7. Her aunt said that she hadn't known him long enough.
8. Her grandfather said that her boyfriend wouldn't be able to support her.
9. She needs her parents' consent, and the minister said that she couldn't get married without her parents' consent.
10. Even the judge said that she needed her parents' consent.

Page 92

2. His father told him not to get married until he had a job.
3. The minister told him not to rush into marriage.
4. His grandfather told him to enjoy himself while he was young.
5. His best friend told him to do what he thought was right.
6. Another friend told him to try to forget Barbara.
7. Barbara's father told him to wait until Barbara was 18.
8. His sister told him not to get married until he was 21.
9. His high school teacher told him to get a college education first.
10. His brother told him to get to know Barbara better before he married her.

Page 93

2. He asked Diane if (whether) she could type.
3. He asked Diane if (whether) she had any office experience.
4. He asked Diane if (whether) she would (she'd) work overtime.
5. He asked her if (whether) she was a high school graduate.
6. He asked her if (whether) she would (she'd) work at night.
7. The interviewer asked her if (whether) she could take shorthand.
8. He asked if (whether) she was a college graduate.
9. The interviewer asked if (whether) she would (she'd) work on Saturdays.
10. The interviewer asked Diane if (whether) she could begin tomorrow.

Page 94

2. He asked Diane how many languages she could speak.
3. The interviewer asked Diane how fast she could type.
4. He asked Diane what college she had graduated from. (He asked Diane what college she graduated from.)
5. He asked her when she had graduated from high school. (He asked her when she graduated from high school.)
6. He asked her how much office experience she had had. (He asked her how much office experience she had.)
7. He asked her how long she had worked for Selby Company. (He asked her how long she worked for Selby Company.)
8. He asked Diane how fast she could take shorthand.
9. He asked Diane why she wanted to work for A.B.C. Company.
10. He asked her when she could begin work.

Page 95

2. I can't believe he asked her if she was happily married.
3. I can't believe he asked her if she had any children.
4. I can't believe he asked her why she didn't have any children.
5. I can't believe he asked her if she was planning on having a family.
6. I can't believe he asked her how much money her husband made.
7. I can't believe he asked her how old she was.
8. I can't believe he asked her what religion she was.
9. I can't believe he asked her what political party she belonged to.
10. I can't believe he asked her if she had any personal problems.

Page 96

2. since
3. For
4. ago
5. for
6. ago
7. since
8. since
9. for
10. For
11. ago
12. for
13. ago
14. since
15. for

Page 97

2. ---
3. to
4. for
5. for
6. ---
7. to
8. ---
9. for
10. for
11. --
12. for
13. ---
14. to
15. to

Page 99

2. in/on
3. at/in
4. at
5. On/on
6. from/to
7. in
8. from/to (until)
9. On
10. in
11. In/on
12. At
13. at/from/to
14. in
15. On/from/to

Page 100

2. at
3. to
4. to
5. about
6. for
7. about
8. for
9. at
10. to
11. at
12. for

Page 101

2. figuring/taking
3. selecting
4. not making
5. guessing
6. not passing
7. failing
8. doing
9. taking
10. not doing

Page 102

2. with
3. at
4. of
5. at
6. of
7. about
8. about
9. of
10. at

Also individual answers.

Page 103

2. finding
3. start
4. move
5. rent
6. spending
7. obtaining
8. work
9. see
10. hearing

Page 104

2. Do you want me to fill it in today?
3. Do you want me to look it up (in the annual report) today?
4. Do you want me to add them up today?
5. Do you want me to write it down today?
6. Do you want me to type it up today?
7. Do you want me to run them off today?
8. Do you want me to hand them out (to all the salespeople) today?
9. Do you want me to call him up today?
10. Do you want me to turn it in (to Mr. Suzuki) today?